EMERSON AND GREENOUGH

TRANSCENDENTAL PIONEERS
OF AN
AMERICAN ESTHETIC

EMERSON
AND GREENOUGH

TRANSCENDENTAL PIONEERS

OF AN

AMERICAN ESTHETIC

CHARLES R. METZGER

UNIVERSITY OF CALIFORNIA PRESS
BERKELEY & LOS ANGELES

1954

University of California Press • Berkeley and Los Angeles
Cambridge University Press • London • England
Copyright 1954 by the Regents of the University of California
PRINTED IN THE UNITED STATES OF AMERICA
DESIGNED BY WARD RITCHIE
L. C. CATALOG CARD NO. 54–10438

ACKNOWLEDGMENT

I should like to thank Mr. Thomas Munro, editor of the *Journal of Aesthetics and Art Criticism,* for permission to reprint here that portion of chapter ii which appeared earlier in the journal. I should like to record also my thanks to publishers for permission to quote from works of which they are the copyright holders: from Emerson's *Complete Works* and *Journals,* to Houghton Mifflin Company, Boston; from F. O. Matthiessen's *American Renaissance,* to Oxford University Press, New York; from Vernon Louis Parrington's *Main Currents in American Thought,* to Harcourt, Brace and Company, New York; and from Lorado Taft's *History of American Sculpture,* to The Macmillan Company, New York. I should like to thank Professors E. H. Eby and D. D. Griffith of the University of Washington for reading various versions of the manuscript several times and for making helpful comments. I should like to thank Mr. Harold A. Small not only for pruning the manuscript where it needed it, but also for contributing valuable references in the notes to Thomas Aquinas, James Fenimore Cooper, William Hogarth, and Francesco Milizia. I should like finally to thank Carol my wife, and my parents Sigrid and Charles F. Metzger, for the support, moral and financial, that they have given to this, my project.

C. R. M.

INTRODUCTION

America may be said to have developed no positive esthetic until the decades preceding the Civil War. Not until the eighteen thirties and forties, when Ralph Waldo Emerson and his friend the sculptor Horatio Greenough began to make themselves heard, was there any dawning of a mature and independent awareness of problems relating to esthetic judgment and artistic performance. Not till then was there any independent examination and criticism of the European arts and esthetic theories which previously Americans had accepted reverently and without question, when not ignoring such matters altogether.

Emerson and Greenough were two of the chief pioneers of this reorientation. They were also pioneers of an organic esthetic in America itself—a branch esthetic, actually, developed in America out of local conditions and running parallel with, rather than subordinate to, a similar organic esthetic developing at the same time in Europe. Their pioneering is important to the history of American esthetics because it marks at least a temporary coming of age in American thought, by virtue of their arriving, more or less independently, at conclusions about art which were on a par with advanced European thought.

This volume is concerned, therefore, with defining the esthetic positions of Emerson and Greenough, and with a rather close comparison of these positions, since though separate they are nevertheless intimately related; it is also concerned with the connections of these positions with the general condition of New England transcendental thought from which they appear to have developed; and it takes into account those religious, scientific, and artistic faiths held by Emerson and Greenough which were conditioned not only by the main trends of New England thought but by European thought as well.

The condition of New England transcendental thought in Emerson's and Greenough's time was one of transition from a predominantly religious concern to one which was essentially secular. As Walt Whitman said of his own time and circumstances, "The priest departs, the divine literatus comes." Applied to Emerson, Whitman's generalization suggests that the departure of the priest and the arrival of the literatus amounted actually to a shift of emphasis in transcendental thought, and that this shift occurred even within the spirit of a single man. It suggests that both the religious aspects and the esthetic aspects of Emerson's thought, and of New England transcendental thought generally, may be viewed profitably together—especially when attention is paid to the relationships between them.

These two aspects have already been studied more or less separately. Vernon Louis Parrington concerned himself chiefly with the religious ones, in his *Main Currents in American Thought;* and F. O. Matthiessen primarily with the esthetic ones, in his *American Renaissance.* Vivian C. Hopkins, in her study of Emerson's esthetic theory, *Spires of Form,* has approached consideration of both, referring on several occasions to Emerson's religious thought in connection with her discussion of his esthetic theory; but she has not concerned herself primarily with comparing them, nor, in her concern with Emerson's esthetic, has she paid much attention to Greenough.

Greenough's writings do not at first glance suggest any obvious connection with the main body of New England transcendental thought. Yet Professor Matthiessen, discussing "The Organic Principle," found Greenough indispensable to an understanding of Emerson's esthetic and included in that chapter of his book an entire section on Greenough, by way of clarifying not only Emerson's position, but the positions of Thoreau, Hawthorne, Melville, and Whitman as well. Clearly, further study of Greenough's esthetic, particularly as it relates to transcendental thought, is in order. Until now, however, no extended study of it has been made.

The present volume is designed to correct in some degree the present incidental and unconnected view of Greenough in the history of American thought. In this book, Greenough's esthetic is not treated incidentally to a study of Emerson's, but rather jointly, in connection with it. Greenough's ideas, as well as Emerson's, are studied against a background of New England transcendental thought, since that thought is as much a part of Greenough's background as it is of Emerson's. As a consequence, Greenough may now be seen to connect more directly with that transcendental tradition which ordered Emerson's thought than has been suspected hitherto.

Both Emerson and Greenough receive, it is hoped, a fair measure of their due as prophets and as pioneers.

CHAPTER
ONE

1. THE TRANSCENDENTAL ESTHETIC

The New England transcendentalists have not generally been looked upon as the founders and champions of an esthetic philosophy in America. They were protestant* ministers, most of them, ostensibly concerned more with man's prospects of salvation than with the contemplation of beauty. Nevertheless, any serious study of New England transcendentalism must take into account the fact that there were two distinct subspecies of transcendentalists: the transcendental ministers, who were not primarily estheticians, and the transcendental

* In this book the terms "protestant" and "protestantism" are not capitalized, because the large letters would appear to indicate a narrower signification than is generally intended. Only on a few pages might they be capitalized to signify a meaning restricted to religious differences only.

poets, who were. It must deal also with the ties by which these two subgroups were intimately related in spite of their major differences.

These relationships are best seen in terms of historical perspective. Today, we may look back upon the New England transcendental movement as one of the chief manifestations of a delayed secularization of New England thought. Walt Whitman referred to it as a change from "priest" to "divine literatus." "Viewed today [1871] from a point of view sufficiently over-arching," he said, "the problem of humanity all over the civilized world is social and religious, and is to be finally met and treated by literature. *The priest departs, the divine literatus comes.*" [1] † Whitman's assessment certainly applies to conditions as they existed in transcendental New England; for, seen from Whitman's overarching point of view, the transcendentalists— Channing, Parker, Emerson, Thoreau (and Whitman himself)—actually do describe the transition he defines.

That it should be interpreted as a manifestation of a secular trend is due primarily to the radical protestant's attitude toward art. The New England transcendentalist's protestant forebears had generally rejected the esthetic on the grounds that it led toward idolatry, since the esthetic, in dealing with form, tends to remove attention from spirit. Radical protestants tended, on the whole, to associate art with what they considered to be "Catholic idolatry." And hence, almost exactly to the degree that medieval Catholicism had

† For notes see pages 137–148 below.

sponsored art, so radical protestantism tended to deny it. Contrary to the Catholic, in whose eyes art is often a useful adjunct to religion, many a protestant saw art, at its very best, to be secular; at its worst, he saw it to be sinful.

In the areas outside New England where the dominion of the church over the rest of society was less absolute—where extreme religious doctrines were taken less seriously, and by a smaller part of the population—the esthetic consciousness of the citizenry was at least not repressed. Often, as in Virginia and in the larger commercial centers, interest in the esthetic was encouraged. But while the rest of American society and intellect was becoming gradually more secular, and more interested in art and beauty, society in New England tended to remain pretty much as it had always been—under the stewardship of its protestant ministry.

It appears likely that it was this delay which brought about, finally, the relatively sudden change of the New England "priest" into the "literatus" and, hence, the rather sudden emergence of a transcendental esthetic strikingly different from the neoclassic esthetic prevalent elsewhere in America; for by the time the New England mind got around to concerning itself with art and beauty, the eighteenth-century neoclassical standards which had impressed themselves upon the rest of American thought had begun to show inherent deficiencies. In arriving late upon the scene, the transcendental esthetician enjoyed the advantage of appearing just in time to lead off in a new direction.

The transcendental esthetic appears to have resulted from little more than a simple extension of the New England Unitarian minister's tendency to apply the devices of philosophical speculation to his consideration of religious matters. This extension, and hence this intrusion of philosophy upon religion in an area such as New England, where doctrinaire Calvinism had from the very beginning reigned supreme, was due, paradoxically, to that very supremacy. In short, the New England ministry had become involved in philosophy by virtue of its own dominion over intellect.[2] The clergy had tended to enlist the best and most active minds for the reason that whenever an institution controls intellect, that institution itself becomes the chief place where intellect is allowed to survive (if at all) and where intellect is encouraged to develop (in the best interest of that institution). However, intellect, if inadequately policed—when freed even partially from the dominion of a parochial or state church, as it was increasingly freed in New England,—is inclined to follow its own courses, whatever may be the proscriptions of its sponsors. Hence, despite the rigidly doctrinaire Calvinism of early New England, some clergymen eventually became more like secular philosophers than priests, for the reason that persons of normally secular philosophical bent, who if living in a secular society would have remained outside the ministry, were, in New England, directed into the church. By the beginning of the nineteenth century, as Professor Parrington has pointed out, many New

England ministers had become more interested in those fundamental religious questions which lead to the study of metaphysics than in administering the ritual, that is, in presiding over the machinery of salvation: "They [the transcendentalists] were all pretty much Unitarians," says Parrington, "and largely clergymen; [and] their primary interest was metaphysical." [3]

As metaphysicians, and hence as philosophers, the transcendental ministers looked out upon the ever-widening world of secular intellect—upon the emergent secular conceptions deriving from science and relating to art, which were extending the boundaries of intellectual inquiry far beyond their own narrow province. Those who had joined the ministry primarily because of the opportunities it offered them for intellectual leadership began to doubt the wisdom of their choice. The transcendental minister-philosopher was not able for long to avoid recognizing that his position as an intellectual leader was somewhat anachronistic.

From this realization descends the main difference between the transcendental priest and the transcendental poet; for whereas the priest contented himself for the most part with looking out upon the new areas of secular thought, the poet insisted upon entering into them. Yet even when he had gone so far as to renounce the clergy, the transcendental poet and philosopher retained much of his clerical attitude. He was not content, as others have been since, to deify science or art, each in its own right. Rather he insisted upon relating science and art to God; and the result of his endeavor to do so is the strange and intimate mixture of religious, scientific, and artistic faiths which characterizes the thought of an Emerson.

2. THE PRIEST BECOMES THE POET

This mixture of faiths will repay examination. But first it will be advisable to scrutinize the transcendental movement in the light of Whitman's statement, "The priest departs, the divine literatus comes"—this, if only to suggest some of the reasons why the transcendental esthetic, and particularly Emerson's esthetic, is complicated and hence difficult to deal with.

Any study of the transcendental movement, any study of the change from priest to literatus, will eventually focus itself upon Emerson. He occupied the central position in time. Coming between Channing and Thoreau, he shared the characteristics of each. Like Channing and Parker, Emerson was a minister; like Thoreau and Whitman, he was a poet-philosopher. And if, as has been suggested, there was a revolution in New England thought, then Emerson was most certainly its chief revolutionary; his actions in that cause are recorded plainly enough in his decisions to leave the ministry and to become a poet.

Yet so gradually did Emerson change from the one position to the other, and so skillfully did he relate his new position to the old one, that the revolutionary nature of his action may easily pass unrecognized. Nor was the smoothness of Emerson's transition achieved by cautious calculation on his part. The transition within his attitude of mind is difficult to see clearly, for two reasons: he never completely abandoned his old attitudes, and his new attitudes were not entirely new.

The transcendental ministers had been, to begin with, a good deal under the influence of the seventeenth-century clerical-literary tradition. They prepared their sermons with care as well as enthusiasm—with an ear for rhythm, balance, and smoothness of delivery which gave to their utterances a style far different from that of the popular rousing eloquence of extempore sermons by preachers like the evangelist Whitefield. Their sermons were in the literary rather than the evangelical tradition, and many of them had real literary value.

The transitions from the published sermon to the published address, to the essay, and to the poem—when the writer is naturally a poet—are gradual and easy, and the collective result of these transitions becomes apparent, and therefore striking, only when the intermediate steps are removed and one is confronted by Whitman the poet as compared with Channing the priest. Even then, to the mind untroubled by partisan loyalty to religious orthodoxy, the contrast is not so great as might be expected. Nearly all will agree that Emerson, Thoreau, and Whitman (although Emerson had left the clergy and although neither Thoreau nor Whitman ever joined it) were as profoundly religious, in the sense of their being interested

in man's spiritual welfare, as were the more orthodox transcendental ministers who preceded them. The
shift from priest to poet was more nearly one of
emphasis than of substance.

Beyond this point, however, Whitman's analysis
ceases to suggest specific relationships and is of further
value only so far as it suggests pertinent questions. It
fails to indicate any of the underlying reasons for what
happened. It is idle, of course, to take Whitman to task
for not suggesting the answer to a question which was
none of his concern. But it is important to recognize
again that the transition from priest to poet, specifically
in New England, signified more than the awakening of
a relatively secular interest in literature, and in art
generally, among ministers whose interests were already
somewhat literary.

Many priests before Emerson, and since, have turned
to the production of literature without feeling obliged
to leave the church. The religious poet is quite obviously not in direct conflict with the priesthood. Hence
the problem becomes: not, Why did Emerson leave
the ministry to become a poet? but rather, Why, concurrent with his becoming a poet, did Emerson conclude to leave the ministry? Beyond the answer to this
question lies the significance of the transcendental
esthetic as well.

It has already been suggested that the transcendentalist's, and thus Emerson's, reasons for leaving the
ministry—as well as his reasons for turning his at-

tention to art and beauty—derived from a growing philosophical concern with areas of intellect beyond the narrow pale of New England theology. Equally it has been suggested that Emerson might conceivably have become a poet without leaving the clergy. But since poetry, and literature in general, tend to serve the "literatus" as a vehicular device for arriving at some more distant end as often as they serve him with a destination or end in itself, an examination of Emerson's purpose as a poet may reveal the beginnings of his transcendental esthetic faith.

Even the briefest examination of his works reveals that Emerson's literary or poetic purpose was not that of the orthodox protestant "literatus." He does not re-tell Scripture; he does not make graphic portrayal of Heaven or Hell. He appears, in fact, to have been concerned more with God's nature than with man's fate. Nevertheless, it is in his poems, essays, and addresses that one finds, variously expressed, his religious conception. Actually, it was his religious conception as much as his literary inclination which divorced him from the clergy and at the same time suggested to him that he should become a poet; for as it developed, his religious conception became broader than even the liberal Unitarian orthodoxy could permit. He left the clergy not simply because he wanted to become a poet, and not, most certainly, because he had become secular in the sense of abandoning his prior religious conviction, but rather because in expanding his religious conception from the level of doctrinal preachment to that of philosophical inquiry he had found the Unitarian orthodoxy lacking in scope.

Already, young Unitarian clergymen had begun not only to examine Divine goodness and truth as available to them in Scripture, but also to approach goodness and truth philosophically, as subjects of inquiry to be pursued independent of Scripture. In so doing they had extended the New England religious conception to its very limits. They had transformed worship into inquiry: they had turned the priest into the scholar, the custodian of divinity into the student of metaphysical and ethical philosophy. Their next step in this direction could only be to complete the trinity by making the priest an esthetic philosopher as well—a worshiper of beauty and perhaps even a practitioner of art. Such was Emerson's office, and in performing it he transformed the priest, if indeed the transcendental worshiper could still be called a priest, not only into an esthetic philosopher but, beyond that, into a poet.

3. A WORSHIPER OF BEAUTY

Like the transcendental ministers who preceded him, Emerson worshiped abstract goodness and truth as aspects of Deity. But, unlike them, he insisted upon worshiping beauty as well—and upon the same terms. Thus, in his essay "The Transcendentalist," he announced: "This class [transcendentalists] are not sufficiently characterized if we omit to add that they are lovers and worshippers of Beauty. In the eternal trinity of Truth, Goodness, and Beauty, each in its perfection including the three, they prefer to make Beauty the sign and head."[4] It is apparent that to Emerson's mind the worship of beauty ranked equal to, if not even above, the worship of goodness and truth.[5] To Emerson, beauty was at least as much an aspect of Deity as were wisdom and morality. And in conceiving thus of beauty, Emerson completed the incorporation of secular philosophy into the New England religious conception. To the metaphysical and ethical provinces already annexed thereto he added the one remaining, the esthetic.

He was wise enough to recognize that in doing so he had overstepped the boundaries of his calling, and honest enough to admit it. Yet he did not recant; he did not turn back. He appears to have thought himself completely justified in extending worship into this new area, and to have set forth in serenity to worship beauty and to consider art. His justification is implicit in his essentially pantheistic conception of Deity. Acceptance or rejection of that concept seems to have determined whether a transcendentalist remained a priest or became a literatus.

There is some question of whether or not Emerson was an out-and-out pantheist, and of whether or not he regarded the universe and the forms of nature literally as corporeal aspects of Deity. It is often possible to substitute the term *Deity* for the term *nature* in Emerson's writings without seriously damaging the sense; yet the fact remains that Emerson had been a minister of the gospel, and it seems doubtful that he would have subscribed to a thoroughgoing, which is to say essentially literal, pantheism. Nevertheless, so far as it affected the rest of his thinking, Emerson's conception of the relationship between Deity and nature remains so much like pantheism as to warrant our giving that name to it for practical purposes of reference. If Emerson did not accept nature as the literal form of Deity, he did see it as "the projection of God" [6]—as "the exposition of God." And when he wished to communicate with Deity, Emerson went to nature. "Nature," he said, "is too thin a screen: the glory of the One breaks through everywhere." [7]

As Emerson himself recognized, to conceive of nature either literally, as God's person, or figuratively, as God's handiwork, is to turn the believer away from the church. To conceive so of nature is to accept tenets inimical to the best interests of a professional clergy operating under the sanctions of an instituted religious orthodoxy; for in accepting nature as an aspect of God's handiwork, the pantheist (even when he does not accept nature as an aspect of God's person) makes Deity available to everyone, and in so doing not only denies the doctrine of grace but also threatens the clergyman with what amounts to technological unemployment. Hence to the transcendentalist more interested in remaining a minister than in becoming an artist, pantheism, even when qualified as was Emerson's, becomes inadmissible. Accordingly, Channing had denounced the pantheistic conception of Deity:

"The doctrine that God is the only Substance, which is Pantheism, differs little from the doctrine that God is the only active power of the universe. . . . One of the greatest of all errors is the attempt to exalt God, by making him the sole cause, the sole agent in the Universe, by denying to the creature freedom of will and moral power, by making man a mere recipient and transmitter of foreign impulse. This, if followed out consistently, destroys all moral connection between God and his creatures . . . it makes the universe a machine." [8]

If Channing argued obliquely, rather than directly, in defense of his position as a professional clergyman, it must be admitted that he recognized for what it was the danger to which his position was exposed by this pantheistic extension of Deity. Emerson himself recorded privately, "To believe too much is dangerous, because it is the near neighbour to unbelief. Pantheism leads to Atheism." [9]

4. PANTHEISM AND PROTESTANTISM

That pantheistic conception of Deity which caused Emerson to abandon his priestly office and become a worshiper of beauty represents one of the final extensions of the protestant religious argument. It includes some of the most powerful premises that have ever been advanced jointly in the name of the protestant individual and against the strictures of institutionalized conduct whether in religion, polity, or art.

Although in recent times religious protestantism has

been responsible for the founding of more separate and warring institutions than perhaps any other single attitude of human faith, the fact remains that the chief arguments of religious protest have always been anti-institutional in tone. Thus the history of protestantism is in essence the history of conflict between the individual and the institution. In practice it has been something more like the history of conflict between the smaller protestant institution and the larger dominant one; but it will be noticed, even in this regard, that whenever the protestant institution succeeds, whenever it either defeats the larger institution or wrings autonomy from it, it ceases correspondingly to be protestant and suffers, in its own turn, protest from dissenting individuals and factions. When followed to its inevitable conclusion, protestantism leads always away from the institution and arrives finally at the basic unit of religious, political, or cultural autonomy, the self-reliant individual. The end of religious protestantism is religious anarchy; or, to use a politer term, religious individualism; and the history of protestant theology is in a large sense the history of argument developed in the interest of the dissenting individual or his group and against the strictures of institutional discipline.[10]

The source of all truly protestant religious argument is the fundamental principle of the individual priesthood of all believers. Taken alone, this concept makes the individual believer the peer of the institution. However, it has seldom been held consistently or alone. Rather it has been employed sparingly, and on occasion only when schismatic elements would publicly separate themselves from the larger sect. Its effect has been consistently that of shifting authority from older, established sources to other, newer ones.

Briefly sketched, the sequence of shifts in religious allegiance leading up to Emerson's pantheism goes somewhat as follows. Discounting those shifts in religious allegiance which occurred when factions were formed in support of warring popes, and discounting the transference of the authority of divine right from papacy to kingship, the first major transference of religious authority in modern times was in the elevation of the Bible above the Roman institution as the final source of religious authority. In transferring authority from the institution to the book, protestantism armed against all comers the individual who could read and interpret what he read. Later, the pietists, by reintroducing the highly emotional device of direct mystical communion with Deity, absolved the believer even from the necessity of learning how to read. On the American frontier, where ministers were few and literacy uncommon, this evangelical appeal to the individual conscience and to the emotions had been wondrously successful. This evangelism (which precipitated "the Great Awakening" in America) had even managed to penetrate the defenses of New England Calvinism.[11]

Among the highly literate Virginia deists and Episcopalians pietism was considerably less successful. In appealing directly to the emotions, in appealing to the spirit and to the private conscience, it gave little opportunity and little justification for displaying skillfully reasoned argument, or fine ritual, or wealth. The pietist's argument, or rather his device of mystical communion, possessed the major advantage that it could render justification for the convictions held by nearly any protestant conscience; but it suffered from several important deficiencies. In the first place, direct mystical communion is difficult to come by, and hence the individual believer often finds it easier to subscribe to Deity through an institution than to work up the religious enthusiasm necessary for direct communion. In the second place, direct mystical communion, even when achieved, is difficult to describe; and the insights attained therefrom are even more difficult to justify— particularly in the eyes of the nonmystic. Judged by earthly standards, mystical insights do not always stand up too well, especially when under bombardment by reasoned argument. In transcendental New England the pietist's highly emotional connection with Deity lacked the permanence and steadiness which could only be secured to it by reasoned argument. In short, although the mystical experience served to emancipate conscience, it failed generally to satisfy intellect.

As a protestant intellectual who nevertheless accepted the pietistic device of direct communion, Emerson must have felt this deficiency rather sharply. "The Transcendentalist," he had said, "adopts the whole connection of spiritual doctrine. He believes in miracle, in the perpetual openness of the human mind to new influx of light and power; he believes in inspiration, and in ecstasy." [12] Carried to extremes, Emerson's pietistic sympathies could lead him only to deny intellect. But Emerson stubbornly refused to be stampeded by the cry of consistency into taking up any such extreme and untenable position; for he was aware that protest unembodied and without support of argument could not very well survive. What Emerson needed, therefore, was a religious conception that could secure for him not only the freedom which communion by conscience had rendered unto the seventeenth-century pietist, but one which might also render unto him the solid support of argument reasoned from evidence, the kind of argument which was the mainstay of eighteenth-century deism.

Emerson's pantheistic, or nearly pantheistic, conception of Deity accomplished exactly this: it qualified the believer both as a communicant and as an observer.[13] What the individual believer could not learn directly from Deity via the mystical experience as interpreted by his own conscience, he could derive indirectly by reasoning from the observations of that conscience in nature. The mystical insight was thus rendered tenable by supporting evidence: not from scriptures or from dogma, but from God's own nature. And the individual believer's conscience was armed, thereby, with not one but two supplemental and hence doubly powerful pieces of critical ordnance to be employed against the institution whenever it displeased him. But as Emerson clearly recognized, and

as his own actions amply illustrate, the believer thus armed against the religious institution ceases almost to be a believer. Instead he becomes an observer and a critic; and critical observation is not judged commonly as an act of faith.

The principal and most immediate effect of the protestant believer's acceptance of a pantheistic, or nearly pantheistic, conception of Deity was the diversion of his attention from consideration of a relatively unembodied deific Spirit to consideration of Deity in terms of objects and phenomena, of forms and principles—these as they were available to the pantheist in nature—seen either as God's very person or at least as His handiwork. In effect, the pantheistic conception of Deity gave form to the deific Spirit, and in so doing it rendered communion more an intellectual and less an emotional process; for although the highly emotional processes of direct communion pertain almost exclusively to the religious experience, the processes of observation apply to other aspects of human experience as well. Observation is a basic device of both science and art; hence, in making the believer an observer as well as a communicant, the pantheist ran the risk of completely transferring his allegiance from religion to science and art. With Emerson and the transcendental literati however, the transference was either so incomplete or so gradual that the effect, as we look back upon it, was a merging of these three faiths—the religious, the scientific, and the artistic—rather than a clearly defined transference from one to another.

But if, in making the religious believer an observer as well as a communicant, Emerson led the believer to concern himself with form as well as spirit, and if by that much he transferred the believer's attention to the provinces of science and art, Emerson also carried with him into those new provinces the general attitudes of protest which had governed his religious conception. In leaving the priesthood and in choosing to worship beauty, Emerson did not by any means cease to be a protestant. In fact, Emerson's worship of beauty cannot truthfully be characterized otherwise than as protestant worship. And his esthetic cannot, by the same token, be reckoned as other than a protestant esthetic.

CHAPTER
TWO

1. AN ESTHETIC PROTESTANTISM

As Emerson himself was aware, the character of protestant argument transcends the boundaries of its particular subject. The protestant argument, on whatever subject, is generally the expression of a particular and often perverse temperament, namely, the protestant temperament. And although, as Emerson points out, there is an identifiable protestant tradition extending throughout history, it is the temperament, primarily, which has kept that tradition alive. The protestant temperament is characterized by an essentially idealistic way of thinking which is at the same time a critical way of thinking. It is critical for the simple reason, as Parrington has stated it, that "communing with the ideal rarely begets complacency." [1]

As an idealist, and as a critic, Emerson identified his own temperament with that of the men who earlier created what may be called the protestant tradition. In his essay "The Transcendentalist" he asserted that his was a way of thinking which, "falling on despotic times, made patriot Catos and Brutuses; falling on superstitious times, made prophets and apostles; on popish times, made protestants and ascetic monks . . . ; on prelatical times, made Puritans and Quakers; and falling on Unitarian and commercial times, makes the peculiar shades of Idealism which we know." [2] This suggests also that Emerson's exact position as an esthetic protestant is ascribable not only to temperament and tradition, but to milieu as well. Indeed, the "Unitarian and commercial" aspects of Emerson's milieu may be seen to suggest respectively the positive and the negative aspects of Emerson's artistic faith—a subject to which we shall return.

For a multitude of reasons, America, right up to Emerson's time, had been the one place where the protestant temperament and tradition was most likely not only to survive but to flourish. Indeed, the protestant temperament had so triumphed here that in Emerson's time the intellect coming to maturity could exercise the freedoms, both religious and political, which the protestant temperament always seeks. They might be incomplete, and their safeguards imperfect, but an optimist such as Emerson could easily find justification for turning the artillery of his protestant argument against some target of larger density than any of those which remained to threaten the exercise of individual judgment in religion or polity.

Only in those cultural provinces which encompassed art and beauty was the American conscience not notably free. Hence it was only natural that a protestant temperament such as Emerson's should turn wholeheartedly to the task of securing for the individual conscience the same freedom from the strictures of institutional guidance with respect to art which it already appeared to enjoy with respect to religion and polity. Professor Matthiessen points out that not only Emerson, but also Hawthorne, Thoreau, Whitman, and Melville, "felt that it was incumbent upon their generation to give [artistic] fulfilment to the potentialities freed by the Revolution, to provide a culture commensurate with America's political opportunity." [3] Particularly among the transcendental poets, an effort was made not only to free America's art and America's judgment of art from the disciplines of the dominant European standards of taste, but also to free the individual American, whether artist or critic, from all rigidly instituted standards of esthetic judgment.

This followed naturally from the transcendental poet's position as a protestant; for if the protestant temperament can so argue as to render the individual judgment free from institutional guidance in religion and polity, if it can make each man's conscience his gospel and each man's person his state, it is equally capable of rendering each man a judge of beauty and a critic of art. It is not surprising, therefore, to discover

that the chief motives and arguments which characterize Emerson's esthetic protest run closely parallel to
the basic arguments and motives which also characterize his religious protest; that at times, in fact, they
are the same. Nor is it surprising to discover that in
worshiping beauty, as in worshiping Deity, Emerson
asserted the competence of the individual judgment;
and that in asserting this right of the individual to
pass his own esthetic judgments, Emerson, as an esthetic protestant, found it as necessary to weaken and
if possible destroy the dominion of institutions over
esthetic experience, as it had been necessary for the
religious protestant to weaken and destroy the dominion of institutions over religious experience. Neither
is it surprising to discover that to this purpose Emerson employed the same pantheistic conception and
argument which had rendered tenable his extreme
position as a religious protestant. Indeed, it was only
natural that Emerson should have endeavored to secure
for his esthetic protest the same advantages which
accrued to his religious argument. It was only natural
also that he should have modeled his campaign against
the institutions which dominated art in his time upon
the very strategy which had ordered his successful
protest against the dominion of institutions over religious experience.

The general strategy of Emerson's esthetic protest,
like that of his religious protest, was one of envelopment. Its device was that of the expanded conception:
he advanced conceptions of Deity and of beauty which

were of greater scope and validity than the conceptions upon which the religious and esthetic institutions of his time were founded. Thus Emerson had confronted the champions of religious orthodoxy with a conception of Deity which was vaster and more expansive than their own; and thus he sought also to confront the custodians of neoclassical taste with a transcendent conception of beauty which would render their conceptions of beauty incomplete by comparison.

In this campaign Emerson derived a great part of his strength from his alliance with nature. As a religious protestant, he had seen fit to expand his conception of Deity to include nature, and in so doing he had come to expand his conception of nature as well. If he tended to look upon phenomenal nature as the corporeal aspect of Deity, he tended, in turn, to look upon Deity as the spiritual aspect of nature. The result was a reciprocal enlargement of both his conceptions. His term *nature* came to mean more than physical nature, and his term *Deity* more than spiritual deity. Indeed, the two terms finally became so large as to mean essentially the same thing, each having assumed the vast compass of the other in addition to its own. As a result, both in Emerson's conception of nature and in his conception of Deity the form and the deific Spirit became united, and each conception came to encompass the whole of the universe both in its real and its ideal aspects.

There were advantages to be derived from these parallel conceptions. The expanded conception of

Deity, including as it did all the phenomena of nature as aspects of Deity, gave the protestant observer a vast supply of evidence from God's handiwork, nature, to be applied in argument against the defenders of orthodoxy. Furthermore, a conception of Deity such as Emerson's, having been expanded to admit evidence from God's nature as at least the equivalent of God's scriptural word, also possessed the advantage that it relieved the religious believer from entering into unequal contest against the ever-extending body of scientific knowledge. One possessing Emerson's vast religious conception was unlikely to feel constrained to take the fundamentalist's suicidal stand against science; rather, he was likely to welcome the scientific method of thinking as a new and extremely useful device to be employed in ascertaining God's truth.

That Emerson included within the framework of his religious conception the chief intellectual device of science, direct observation of nature, is important, particularly in relation to his contingent conception of beauty; for it is Emerson's inclusion within his conception of beauty of major elements descending from both his theological and his scientific convictions regarding nature which accounts for much of the confusion, and nearly all the strength, of his esthetic position.

2. A RELIGIOUS CONCEPTION OF BEAUTY

Since a conception of beauty is as much the basis of esthetic conviction as a conception of Deity is the basis of religious faith, it is necessary to preface an evaluation of the main body of Emerson's esthetic faith with some prior assessment of his conception of beauty.

Emerson's conception of beauty, like his conception of Deity, was expansive; so expansive, in fact, that it assumed proportions as vast, almost, as those of his conceptions of Deity and of nature. It will be remembered, in this regard, that Emerson conceived of beauty as one of the "eternal trinity" of Goodness, Truth, and Beauty, which, when joined together, form the One; and it will be remembered further that Emerson considered each of these three in its perfection to include the other two. This is to say, of course, that beauty, or goodness, or truth—any one of them—in its perfection approximates Deity. In view of this connection, and in view of the fact that to Emerson's mind the terms *Deity* and *nature* existed very nearly as synonyms, it is not surprising to discover that Emerson asserted beauty to be not only a major aspect of Deity, but a major aspect of God's handiwork (nature) as well. "In nature," said Emerson, "all is beautiful." [4]

Indeed, Emerson took nature as both author and model of beauty: as the author of beauty, using the term *nature* in its deific sense, meaning God; and as the model of *beauty*, using that term in its phenomenal sense, meaning the objects which constitute the out-of-doors. The preachment which follows from this identification of beauty with nature and with Deity is, patently, that the worshiper of beauty should not seek inspiration among the arts of the ancients, nor from the

custodians of an established antiquarian esthetic tradition, but rather that, in seeking inspiration, he should
look directly to nature.

This last assertion, supported by the connection
made by Emerson between beauty, nature, and Deity,
gave a moral sanction—indeed, an unimpeachable
respectability—to the protestant esthetic argument. It
gave to the minister turned esthetic philosopher the
comforting assurance of knowing that in the last analysis he was investigating Deity. Its over-all effect,
furthermore, was not only that of freeing the protestant
esthetician from the strictures of clerical orthodoxy in
order that he might worship beauty and study art, but
also that of freeing him from the strictures of such
authority as dominated art in his day. It gave him the
same dialectical advantage over orthodoxy instituted in
the realm of art as the doctrine of individual priesthood, supported by a similar connection of nature with
Deity, had given to the protestant religious believer in
his argument against instituted religious orthodoxy.

This dialectical advantage was twofold. It not only
gave the sanction which adheres among the pious to
any investigation of the nature of God, but it provided
as well the kind of material for argument which is most
likely to convince the essentially skeptical, scientific
mind. For in conceiving of beauty, nature, and Deity
as equivalents, or as near-equivalents, Emerson succeeded effectively in transferring that powerful protestant armament which derived from his religious conception to the arsenal of his esthetic conception. Thus

equipped, he could expect to enjoy, as an esthetic protestant, the same dialectical advantages that had secured his position as a religious protestant.

Moreover, the advantages accruing to an expansive conception of beauty such as Emerson's were practical. Taking as his models the forms of nature rather than the forms of antiquarian art, Emerson was required by their greater number to evolve a larger and hence more widely valid conception of beauty than that advanced by the custodians of a neoclassical esthetic conception. Indeed, his conception of beauty ought to have been superior to that of the neoclassicist—as in fact it was— if only by virtue of the fact that his approach to beauty through the forms of nature required him to contrive esthetic principles which covered vastly greater numbers of specific instances.

More significant, however, than the increase in mere numbers of objects was the addition in kind. For whereas the objects of ancient art (paintings, sculptures, architectural achievements) with which the neoclassicist had concerned himself in developing his conception of beauty had been almost exclusively inanimate, the objects which Emerson consulted in nature (plants, animals, rocks) included not only inanimate but organic or animate objects as well.

It does not appear to make much difference, upon first consideration, whether the philosopher bases his esthetic conception upon an excellent statue of a man or upon the man himself. There is, admittedly, more to be learned about the specific techniques of sculpture from looking at the statue than from looking at the man. But on the high esthetic level at which Emerson operated the advantage is reversed. At that level the difference between observing the statue and observing the man becomes the difference between formulating an esthetic conception which is static and formulating one which is dynamic.

In deriving a major part of his total conception of beauty from his observation of phenomenal nature, Emerson came inevitably to see beauty in terms of the same flux that characterizes the numberless phenomena which constitute nature, and therefore to see nature, and hence beauty, not as fixed or static, but rather as dynamic or flowing. "Beauty," he said, "is the moment of transition, as if the form were just ready to flow into other forms." [5] To Emerson, as to nearly all men, the most fascinating features of this natural flux appeared in relation to the phenomena of growth and apparent adaptation. These features he applied directly to his conception of beauty. "In nature," he said, "all is useful, all is beautiful. It is therefore beautiful because it is alive, moving, reproductive . . ." [6]

Apparently as a result of observing this utility among growing natural (which is to say beautiful) forms, Emerson came to conceive of what amounts to an economical aspect of beauty. "There is not a particle to spare in natural structures," [7] he observed; and he concluded accordingly: "Beauty rests on necessities. The line of beauty is the result of perfect economy." [8] Indeed, the upshot of Emerson's turning directly to phenomenal nature for aid in formulating his conception of beauty was his inclusion of this dynamic-economical assertion—an assertion which extended his esthetic conception beyond those essentially static conceptions of proportion and balance which characterized the neoclassic esthetic. At no time, however, did Emerson deny the esthetic validity of the neoclassic conceptions of proportion and balance. He accepted and espoused them. His argument with the neoclassicists took the form merely of an assertion that conceptions of that kind were not enough. He asserted that not only proportion and balance, but also "every necessary or organic action pleases the beholder." [9]

The general effect was one of activating what previously had been a static conception of beauty. The implications were as revolutionary, and were to be as far-reaching in regard to esthetic conception, as those of Lamarck and Darwin in regard to cosmo-biological conception. Even the immediate effect was an extending of esthetic speculation beyond the narrow pale of New England esthetic conception into broad new areas seldom touched upon before.

But if Emerson's expanded conceptions of Deity and of beauty afforded to his protestant temperament great practical as well as dialectical advantages, they also brought with them at least two major difficulties, one semantic, the other logical. Both attended upon Emerson's using the device of the expanded conception, and both descended either directly or indirectly from Emerson's unitarian religious conviction; for although the advantages in equating Deity with the major terms of one's conceptual vocabulary are very great, such advantages may easily be lost among the vastness of the conceptions to which they accrue. The idea of a universe in which all major aspects equate with the One may be good theology, but it is bad semantics.

Semantically it is extremely dangerous to equate all or nearly all the major terms of one's vocabulary with Deity, for to do so is to equate the terms with each other. Equated thus, they come to suggest essentially the same thing, namely, God; and the reasons for their separate identities tend to disappear. It is therefore difficult to isolate, to apprehend, the ideas of a man such as Emerson, who uses a vocabulary freighted with cosmically expansive terms. And it is even more difficult to discuss these ideas once they are apprehended, since the character of their terminology tends to introduce the investigator into a vast cycle of mutually inclusive terms, each one suggesting another, equally vast, equally important term, *ad infinitum.*

Hence, although Emerson's device of expanded conception (his device of relating all the major terms of his vocabulary to Deity) tended to confound his opponents and perhaps to soothe his Christian conscience, it tended also to confuse his argument and thereby to obscure its great strength. For example, in expanding his conception of nature, Emerson gathered to that term a great number of essentially different meanings. In his writings, *nature* means variously man, not-man, not-society, out-of-doors, essence, universe, and God;

and thus, unfortunately, in failing to distinguish his one use of the term from another, Emerson not only expanded his conception but also confused its exposition. The investigator of Emerson's ideas on beauty, for example, is forced to reconstruct largely from context and from the minor terms of Emerson's vocabulary the vast design of his conception.

Emerson's exposition of his philosophical position is further complicated because, in gathering both God and nature—both the deific Spirit and the form—to the support of his esthetic protest, he brought immediately into focus a major conflict between his conception of the ideal and his observation of the real. As a protestant religious believer—as a Unitarian—Emerson had asserted the existence of a oneness, or unity, within God's universe. But as a pantheist—as a more or less scientific observer—he had also asserted the need of consulting the diverse facts of God's nature in the process of apprehending God's truth. But the oneness of God's universe is not manifestly apparent among the diverse forms of God's nature. Emerson's appeal to nature, then, failed to support the fundamental assertion of religious faith which it might have been expected to confirm.

Emerson was too honest and too clear-sighted, on the one hand, to deny his observations of diversity among natural forms; on the other, he was too deeply religious to deny the validity of his unitarian assertion. At the same time, he could not well leave unresolved this lack of accord between these two fundamental aspects of his religious-esthetic conception; to have done so would have been to leave undefended a major breach in his philosophical position. He resolved the conflict and closed the breach by turning to what was perhaps the only source of argument left to him: he turned to the mind, which embraces both religious and scientific conceptions and which perceives both unity and diversity. "Observe," he said, "this invincible tendency of the mind to unify. It is a law of our constitution that we should not contemplate things apart without the effort to arrange them in order with known facts and ascribe them to the same law." [10] Elsewhere in his *Journal* he referred to "Unity! Unity!" as "the Niagara currents in the mind." [11] And again, in his *Journal,* he said, "To seek the Unity is a necessity of the mind; . . . we do not *choose* to resist duality, complexity." [12]

It had become apparent to Emerson that the mind's perception of unity was at least as much a matter of God's will with regard to the mind as it was a matter of the mind's independent recognition of order and unity actually present in God's handiwork, nature. Emerson came therefore to see the vast diversity of facts in God's nature as the raw material with which intellect deals. "The Mind," said Emerson, "must think by means of Matter; find Matter or Nature the means and words of its thinking and expression." [13] In his essay on "Beauty" he announced: "All the facts in nature are nouns of the intellect, and make the grammar of the eternal language. . . . And there is a joy in perceiving the representative or symbolic character of a fact, which no bare fact or event can ever give." [14] In pursuit of that line of thought he came to realize that the mind's perception, or more accurately the mind's conception, of several objects or phenomena as united (as well as the mind's conception of an object or phenomenon as single and of itself) represents primarily the employment of a certain way of looking at nature, or Deity. Thus he began to see the assertions of his own unitarian faith within the framework of their psychological functions as devices of intellect.

As a result of this insight, it became unnecessary for Emerson to prove either that unity was not an identifiable aspect of nature, or that it was; for whether there exists a "real" unity running through the divine mind, behind nature, and perceivable by the mind of man, or whether unity exists solely as a conception within the human mind, the validity of Emerson's unitarian assertion remains the same. In short, by conceiving of unity as a device of the mind, Emerson made it unnecessary to deny the possibility that there might be no "real" relationship of unity among the forms of God's nature. And thus he accomplished the no small task of rendering previously conflicting elements of his philosophical conception amenable. He had made of man's conception of unity a device whereby intellect comprehends the diversity of natural forms without at the same time denying the original status of "unity" as the inexplicable oneness behind all diversity.

In explaining away the apparent conflict between his assertion of unity and his observation of diversity,

Emerson secured that assertion of unity against the most embarrassing evidence (of diversity) that could be brought against it. And it was absolutely necessary for him to do this. It will be remembered that the entire strategy of Emerson's protest, both in religion and in art, was one of expansive envelopment. He had acted to defeat his adversaries by envisioning unities greater than those which limited their own conceptions. Thus he enveloped them; and thus, for Emerson to have abandoned his expansive unitarian religious conception —even in gaining the support of scientific evidence— would have been equal to abandoning his entire argument; for that conception was fundamental to the entire body of his protestant argument, regardless of subject. As to his esthetic protest in particular, it will be seen that Emerson's unitarian assertion and conception not only ordered his conception of beauty, but actually constituted the positive aspect of his esthetic faith.

Emerson's clearest enunciation of this positive aspect occurs, rightly enough, in his essay on "Beauty." But even in that essay he avoided actually defining the term. "I am warned," he said, "by the ill fate of many philosophers not to attempt a definition of Beauty." [15] He was aware that to define his term was to limit its conception in the minds of his readers; and this, above all else, he sought to avoid, both in the interest of his protestant strategy and in the interest of literal accuracy. His conception of beauty was too vast to be fitted conveniently within the limits of any one definition. For purposes of discussion, however, he was will-

ing to "enumerate a few of its qualities." Thus he said,
"We ascribe beauty to that which is simple; which has
no superfluous parts; which exactly answers its end;
which stands related to all things; which is the mean of
many extremes." [16]

It is important to note, here, that Emerson is describing not things which are beautiful, but those characteristics which the mind conceives as beautiful; and further, that in describing these characteristics Emerson
is actually enumerating psychological devices of esthetic perception. He is saying, in effect, that the mind
conceives of beauty in terms of three kinds of unity (or
simplicity), of which one is static, one dynamic, and
the last cosmic.

Even if Emerson's conception of beauty cannot be
reduced to his conception of unity (or simplicity), or
exactly equated with it, the fact remains that the first
of these conceptions is ordered by the second. Indeed,
a conception of unity, or simplicity, may be seen to
underlie and to order nearly every esthetic. Man's longing for order, for unity, for simplicity—his desire to
live in an explicable universe—is perhaps the motivat-
ing force behind all intellect, whether it is concerned
specifically with religion, with science, or with art. And
perhaps the only valid measure of intellectual attainment, whether in science, religion, or art, lies in the
degree to which intellect has succeeded in reconciling
the mind's longing for simplicity with the observably
diverse facts of life. Emerson's conception of beauty

appears superior, in this regard, to that of the neo-classical estheticians for the very reason that his is based upon a vaster, more flexible conception of unity —of beauty—than theirs; it is one which illumines a greater number of diverse phenomena with the bright beam of interpretation.

The neoclassicist's conception of beauty was ordered primarily by his recognition of the static unities of pro-portion and correspondence, as exemplified on the one hand by the abstractions of Euclid and on the other by such imitations of nature or of ancient art as plainly show rather exact correspondence with their models. The applications to art deriving from such conceptions of unity and beauty are vast, as the great variety and number of them in neoclassical art attest; but such applications are limited, nonetheless, in comparison with those deriving from Emerson's transcendental conception of beauty.

Emerson's own assertion that "we ascribe beauty to that which is simple" concerns these static conceptions of unity chiefly. His statement suggests that the mind takes pleasure in contemplating, for example, a per-fectly smooth stone perceived exclusively as a smooth stone and not as a complex organization of surfaces and chemical elements or in terms of nebulae of positive and negative electrical charges. In this same sense, the mind derives perhaps even greater pleasure from con-templating a perfect sphere formed by craft to an abstract simplicity actually beyond nature's own. Similarly does the mind enjoy perceiving the abstract sim-plicities of balance, of proportion, and of imitative correspondence.

The mind takes pleasure, however, in observing other unities than those of proportion and correspond-ence. Emerson's announcement, for example, that beauty pertains to that "which has no superfluous parts; which exactly answers its end" [17] leads beyond this static conception of unity to one which is dynamic. As a result of looking to nature for aid in developing his esthetic conception, Emerson had perceived there, among its organic forms, an apparent union of the form with its functions—a union which he admitted, entire, into the main body of his conception of unity and beauty. In thus recognizing that "every necessary or organic action pleases the beholder" he added a whole new dynamic conception of unity and beauty to that static conception which he had inherited from the neo-classic esthetic tradition, and along with it a whole new area of consideration to be taken into account by both artist and critic. As will be seen presently, this new area of consideration necessitated an entire metaphysics of art, which is to say a whole new assessment of the creative process. The over-all effect of Emerson's ac-ceptance of this new dynamic-organic conception of unity was that of transferring critical judgment beyond the assessment of an art form in relation to the object or proportion which it imitated to a larger assessment of that form in relation to the functions it performed.

Finally, in asserting that beauty pertains to that

which is "standing in relation to all things; which is the mean of many extremes" Emerson arrived at what amounted to an even broader extension of his conception of unity, a cosmic conception wherein each object fixed by the mind's focus of attention is seen not only in terms of proportion and of purpose but also in relation to the ultimate unity, God. "Every object," said Emerson in this regard, "has its roots in central nature, and may of course be so exhibited to us as to represent the world." [18] This "new virtue which constitutes a thing beautiful," he said, "is a certain cosmical quality, or a power to suggest relation to the whole world, and so lift the object out of a pitiful individuality." [19]

The immediate effect of such a threefold conception applied to the perception of beautiful objects is to require of the observer of beauty and the creator of art that they contemplate each beautiful object with an eye not only to proportion and function, but also to the entire universe. Its effect is to require of the artist and the critic an almost unreasonably broad approach to beauty and art, one approximately as vast as Emerson's own.

But for Emerson, at least, this broad new conception had its advantage. By his conception of unity and of beauty, he was able in subsequent argument to join art with nature and with Deity and to elevate the true artist and the true critic to the level of the priest and seer. His cosmic conception of unity had the further practical advantage—with regard specifically to art— that it released the artist from the bonds of a literal conception of simplicity or unity: the artist, though committed to the task of simplifying human experience, was not required to remain on the level of primitive art; he was allowed to generalize, to reveal entire networks of relationships, all leading to the One. Indeed, it appears that Emerson's inclusion of this cosmic conception of unity within his conception of beauty was due as much to his recognition of the danger that art might descend to, or remain at, the level of primitive unities, as it was to his desire to see art related to Deity. "The balance must be kept,—the power to generalize and the power to individualize must coexist," he said, "to make a poet." [20]

Taken as a whole, Emerson's threefold conception of beauty—in terms of static unity, of dynamic or organic unity, and of cosmic unity—equipped him with an ability to perceive beauty far subtler than that which the art of his day was able to provide. That art was derived from a conception of beauty which included, even at best, little more than a third of the qualities of unity by which Emerson judged a thing beautiful. The unities of the neoclassic, antiquarian art of Emerson's day were the static unities of proportion and correspondence. The conception of a dynamic union of form with function, although it had undoubtedly occurred even to the mind of the neoclassical artist, was not held foremost therein. Among neoclassical artisans, proportion, not function, was God. Even in its cosmic extension the neoclassical conception of design was static. The neoclassicist conceived of the universe in terms of a gigantic watch; and this conception, although it accounted adequately for motion in the cosmos—in nature,—did not account adequately for evolutionary growth and development; the watch runs, but it does not grow.

Naturally, then, in measuring the art of his day by the rule of his vast, dynamic esthetic conception, Emerson found more disappointment than satisfaction. Indeed, only the forms of nature's art appeared to fulfill all the requirements of Emerson's esthetic conception; and he concluded, accordingly, that there was something wrong with man's art.

3. A CRITICISM OF ART

The chief trouble with art in his day, as Emerson saw it, lay not in its execution but in its conception. This is to say that he saw it to be deficient primarily because the conception of beauty behind it was limited by a reliance upon models from ancient art, and consequently had become separated from nature—from the source and model of all true beauty. Separated from nature, art had also become separated from God; and thus separated, it had surrendered up all its authority and all its veracity. "The indisposition of men to go back to the source and mix with Deity," said Emerson, "is the reason of degradation and decay." [21]

Man's art was less that nature's, Emerson observed, because it was not united with nature (and with God). "Now men do not see nature to be beautiful, . . ." he said. "Thus is art vilified; the name conveys to the mind its secondary and bad senses; it stands in the imagination as somewhat contrary to nature, and struck with death from the first." [22] If the artist looked to nature at all, he did so primarily because the ancients had done so. Antiquity, rather than nature, was his model.

Emerson objected to this neoclassical, or antiquarian, conception of beauty not only because it divorced art from nature, but because it was connected with commerce. As a clergyman, Emerson had deplored man's preoccupation with the material aspects of life—with commerce and with the collecting of material wealth to the neglect of spirit. Equally, as an esthetician, he complained that "men seem to have lost the perception of the instant dependence of form upon soul." [23] He saw art too close to commerce and too far removed from spirit.

He was aware that not only neoclassical art but also its early romantic extensions were direct manifestations of that antiquarian-historical point of view which had emerged in full force during the eighteenth century; aware, too, that that point of view had been introduced, and to a degree kept alive, by commerce. He saw that despite the enlargement of local conceptions of beauty and art attendant upon the importation of strange art forms from distant areas, the immediate effect, particularly when the foreign forms were superior to those of the local arts, was a transferring of artistic attention from the creation of original forms to the imitation of imported ones; and that a further effect was the transference of esthetic judgment away from the individual artist and critic to the merchant-importer, or, at best, to the antiquarian scholar.

Indeed, right up to Emerson's own time the antiquarian had exercised virtually undisputed stewardship over all the vast areas of esthetic judgment; he had become, in effect, the high priest of art. Emerson protested against the dominion of that priesthood. "Art is cant and pedantry," he said; "it is not practical and moral, . . . if it do not make the poor and uncultivated feel that it addresses them also." [24] Esthetic truth, as much as religious truth, Emerson believed, must be freely available to the common man without benefit either of erudition or of clergy.

He charged, therefore, that the initial advantage which the neoclassicist had derived in enlarging his esthetic conception by consulting models taken from ancient art had given way immediately to the enslavement of contemporary art. "We are bound hand and foot," he said, "with our decorums and superstitions. England has achieved respectability at what a cost! America with a valet's eyes admires and copies in vain. Art requires a living soul." [25] Thus he charged not only that neoclassical or antiquarian art was unfree; he charged also that it was dead. He had a strong case for his argument. The forms and disciplines of neoclassical art, and of antiquarian art generally, were derived, after all, from the art of dead men. They represented ancient art, exhumed—or perhaps restored—but dead nonetheless.

The chief reason, however, for Emerson's assertion

that art in his day was dead, lifeless, sterile, derived from his comparison of it with nature's art. Along with the natural scientists of his day, he saw that many if not all of nature's forms grew out of their several functions; and he had hoped accordingly to see the forms of man's art similarly derived in terms of their functions. But in examining the art of his day he perceived only that its forms served relatively trivial, and even ignoble, functions. Art served history and commerce. Its forms were no more than symbols of man's regard for antiquity and wealth. In his essay on "Art" Emerson announced that "the whole extant product of the plastic arts has . . . its highest value *as history*." [26] He did not deny the validity of the historical point of view; he employed it himself in the same essay, in which he announced that, "historically viewed, it has been the office of art to educate the perception of beauty." [27] Nevertheless, Emerson did complain against the complete dominion of a historical point of view over art.

In essence, Emerson's complaint was that the historical point of view tends to defeat art's true purpose. Art, in Emerson's day, did not, to his way of thinking, educate the perception of beauty, but rather the perception of history and the appreciation of wealth. A perception of history, if pursued far enough, might lead eventually to a consideration of nature—to the history of nature. But the other function had no such saving grace. Fine art in Emerson's day—whether imported bodily from the areas of antiquity, or merely copied—

had little to recommend it except as it symbolized that there were Americans rich enough to buy it. True, the forms of antiquarian art might serve real functions. The form of the Grecian temple shelters the banker from rain perhaps as effectively as that of any other structure. The Kalevala rhythms and the heroic couplet may serve the poet adequately enough as vehicles for the stuff of his poetry. The point, however, is that these forms were employed less for their actual usefulness than for their relation to antiquity. And the final effect of this employment was akin to that "conspicuous consumption" which Thorstein Veblen was later to denounce. Thus Emerson complained in his day that "art makes the same effort which a sensual prosperity makes; namely to detach the beautiful from the useful." [28]

To Emerson's way of thinking, detaching the useful from the beautiful was tantamount to divorcing art from nature, and, to that extent, from Deity. It had become apparent to him that the only manner in which man might relate his art to nature (and to God), other than by direct representation, was, through employing the analogy of growth, by creating art forms in terms of the natural principles of growth and adaptation; in short, by consciously relating the various forms of art to their more significant functions. Emerson wished, therefore, to see beauty sprung from utility, to see the form of beauty prescribed by the mold of function. Accordingly he asserted in his essay on "Art" that "beauty must come back to the useful arts, and the distinction between the fine and the useful arts be forgotten." [29]

The function of art in general, as Emerson saw it, was to educate man in the perception of beauty. To his mind, that perception meant not only the perception of unity in, or with, God's nature, but ultimately the contemplation of the One, of Deity itself. So far as Emerson could see, art in his day served none of these ends. Neither in representing man's awareness of history nor in representing man's success at acquiring wealth could Emerson see that art suggested either Deity or nature; hence he was unable to conclude otherwise than that "the fountains of invention and beauty in modern society are all but dried up." [30]

There was much to justify that conclusion. By Emerson's time, the chief devices of the neoclassical or antiquarian esthetic had been overexercised: imitation had been carried to excess, and the supply of importations was nearing exhaustion. There were among the areas of ancient Greece and Rome only a limited number of ruins, which is to say only a limited number of art forms to be transported either bodily or by means of imitation into western Europe and America. Even when the legitimate areas of antiquity were extended, as the preromantics extended them, to include every conceivably exotic area, age, and culture, the variety of forms remained nonetheless limited; and their employment in modern society remained primarily that of static or nonfunctional embellishment.

There was a tendency, furthermore, among practitioners of antiquarian art to introduce elements copied from several different areas and ages simultaneously, for the adornment of modern society. The result was an artistic hodgepodge existing in violation apparently of all three of the qualities of unity which Emerson ascribed to the beautiful. As viewed by supporters of the antiquarian esthetic tradition, these mixtures of forms no doubt exerted the appeal of virtuosity. But viewed as Emerson viewed them, in terms of his organic conceptions of unity and beauty, they served only to illustrate the deficiencies of the esthetic behind them.

Excess in art, as in any other aspect of human affairs, serves oftenest to cover up deficiency; and Emerson the observer was not long in apprehending the deficiencies covered by the excesses of antiquarian art. What was the antiquarian artist to do when there should arise in modern society a new activity or function for which none of the ancient cultures had provided a form? The neoclassical esthetic conception was apparently incapable, by itself, of adjusting art to new needs, of making or keeping man's art a living art, in the same sense as nature's art. It was incapable of evolving truly new forms, for the simple reason that it was both static and derivative. Its devices were unable to provide adequately for the esthetic needs of an expanding society.

In looking to nature, however, Emerson had apprehended a new device to be applied to the artistic process, one which was dynamic rather than static, one which might direct art forms into a proper relationship with natural forms. He came to see art, like nature, in terms of creation rather than of imitation. "Art is the need to create," he said. "Nothing less than the creation of man and nature is its end." [31] Emerson came, in effect, to concern himself with what amounted to a metaphysics of art: with the origin and processes of art, both man's and nature's.

4. A METAPHYSICS OF ART

As we have already noted, Emerson came finally to conceive of art as nothing less than "the creation of Beauty." [32] Such was God's art, nature; and such, to his mind, should be man's art. Yet Emerson saw man's art in his day to be divorced from nature—to be imitative rather than creative. He saw man's art serving ignoble employment, and he protested, accordingly, that "there is higher work for Art than the arts. They are abortive births of an imperfect or vitiated instinct." [33] In art, said Emerson, "not imitation but creation is the aim." [34]

In view of his new esthetic insight—as a result of his perceiving intimations of a new artistic process in the workings of nature—Emerson came to deny the sacred theory of the Golden Age which had dominated European art since before the Renaissance. He came to consider undue reverence for the ancients as a sign of esthetic cynicism. "He has conceived meanly of the resources of man," said Emerson, "who believes that the best age of production is past." [35] He held this particular belief accountable for the low condition of art in his time—indeed, for the fact that art was imitative rather than creative. Yet he added, with characteristic optimism, that although the art of his day was at so low an ebb, "a true announcement of the law of [artistic] creation, if a man were found worthy to declare it, would carry art up into the kingdom of nature, and destroy its separate and contrasted existence." [36]

The framing of such an announcement, Emerson considered to be the chief duty of the artist in his time. It was not an easy task, since it had to include an exposition of the chief secrets not only of nature but of the mind as well. He said of it in his *Journal:* "The artist now should draw men together by praising Nature, show them the joy of naturalists in famous Indian glens,—natural botanic gardens,—in the profusion of new genera, . . . Let him unroll the earth and sky, and show the splendor of colour and of form; *then let him, on the top of this delight, add a finer, by disclosing the secrets of intellectual law;* tell them a secret that will drive them crazy; and things that require no system to make them pertinent, but make everything else impertinent." [37]

Emerson's concern with art, like his concern with beauty, the product of art, led him back not only to nature but ultimately to the mind, since it is the mind which both perceives nature and creates art. Initially, however, his concern with the problem of creating beauty, and thus of relating man's art to nature, had led Emerson to consider the probable history and development of the forms of man's art out of his immediate environment in nature. Thus in his essay on "History" he had tentatively suggested that perhaps "by surrounding ourselves with the original circumstances we invent anew the orders and the ornaments of architecture." [38] Thus, to his mind, it was the "snow-drift along the sides of the stone wall which obviously gave the idea of the common architectural scroll to abut a tower." [39] "The Gothic church," he said, "plainly originated in a rude adaptation of the forest trees." [40] He had suggested also that the great arts of antiquity had developed from prior arts fashioned among primitive circumstances in nature; "the Doric temple," he wrote, "preserves the semblance of the wooden cabin in which the Dorian dwelt. The Chinese pagoda is plainly a Tartar tent." [41] But assertions like these are much more nearly products of conjecture than of observation. Stimulating as they must have been to the mind of the poet, they provided little of value to the mind of the esthetic philosopher in search of a satisfactory metaphysics of art. In looking to nature and primitive circumstance as sources of artistic form, Emerson succeeded only in suggesting that much of man's art appears to have been copied—that man's art is, in large part, the product of an essentially literal imitativeness: first, of natural forms, and subsequently, of other art forms.

Thus, in looking to the history of art, literally in terms of nature, Emerson came upon no real assessment of how the artist creates the beauty embodied in his art. And thus, finally, in his concern with the metaphysics of art—in his concern with the processes and with the origins of processes involved in creating art—

Emerson turned, as in his assessment of beauty, away from the literal forms of phenomenal nature to the mind which perceives those natural forms and which is capable not only of perceiving beauty in nature but also of creating beauty in art. He became aware, at last, that investigating the relationships between nature and art might well be less a matter of pushing back beyond the history of art into the most primitive eras of artistic creation, and more one of exploring the mind as it has dealt with art in all times.

Emerson's assertion that "Art is the creation of Beauty" must inevitably have led him to apply to his theory of art the same psychological insights which ordered his conception of beauty. Had he possessed an "orderly" mind, he might have been more forcibly impressed by the significance of his own conclusions; and he might therefore have been stimulated to present his ideas more carefully than he did. But even though his exposition of his attitudes toward art and beauty is jumbled, Emerson was more than vaguely aware of the parallel operations of the mind in perceiving beauty among objects already extant and in envisioning beauty as the theme or purpose behind any creative or artistic work.

He was aware that the secrets both of nature and of the mind lay beyond the realization that the mind operates, both in considering nature and in considering itself, not only in terms of unities or foci of attention but ultimately in terms of the more complex manifestations of this tendency to unify which are known as principles or laws. He was convinced, accordingly, that nature's laws were equally the laws of the human mind; that the two were, in effect, synonymous. "But what," he asked, in "The American Scholar," "is classification [of facts in nature] but the perceiving that these objects are not chaotic, and are not foreign, but have a law which is also a law of the human mind?" [42] This being so, the best way for him to learn how the mind creates the forms of its art lay in observing the creation of forms in nature, and not in examining the production of ancient artists.

Emerson saw nature as "an endless combination and repetition of a very few laws." [43] He saw furthermore that "every principle [perceivable in nature] is an eye [for the mind] to see with. Facts in thousands of the most interesting character," he said, "are slipping by me every day unobserved, for I see not their bearing, I see not their connexion. I see not what they prove." [44] It was in the light of one or more of these principles, or devices of intellect, that Emerson hoped to illumine art. He hoped, in effect, to see the creation of art, like the operations of nature, reduced to "a very few laws." Man might create new forms in art more efficiently, he surmised, by observing and following the laws which appear to govern the creation of new forms in nature; for man's art, like nature's, he was convinced, was more than mere repetition of forms. Thus in a *Journal* entry, under the heading "Art," he had noted: "Two things in picture: (1) Representation of Nature, which a photograph gives better than any pencil, and a *camera obscura* better than a photograph, and which is a miracle of delight to every eye. (2) An ideal representation, which, by selection and much omission, and by adding something not in Nature, but profoundly related to the subject, and so suggesting the heart of the thing, gives a higher delight, and shows an artist, a creator." [45] He came to believe that the creation of true beauty in art, just as the framing of valid interpretations of purpose or design in nature, was intellectual chiefly, and was the product primarily of free, even independent, thought rather than of unquestioning conformance with fixed standards of taste and opinion. "The measure in art and in intellect is one," he wrote. "The very definition of art is, the inspiration of a just design working through all the details. But the forsaking the design to produce effect by showy details is the ruin of any work. Then begins shallowness of effect; intellectual bankruptcy of the artist." [46] All this is to imply, simply, that the more deeply the artist thinks upon his subject the more valid becomes his art.

Perhaps the deepest, certainly the most spectacular and revolutionary, thinking of Emerson's day was in the fields of the emergent natural-biological sciences. It is no wonder, therefore, that he turned for guidance and support to the scientists' observations and interpretations of nature. And thus it was that he succeeded in supporting his assertion of the esthetic validity of unity, in its economical aspect, by arguing that " 'tis a law of botany that in plants the same virtues follow the same forms . . . all beauty must be organic; . . . outside embellishment is deformity." [47]

It is perhaps impossible to tell exactly to what degree Emerson's esthetic theory was influenced by his communing directly with nature, and to what degree it was conditioned by his reading in the scientific literature of his time.[48] Perhaps a precise measure of these two influences is not too important. It is important, however, to bear in mind that Emerson was exposed to the scientific theorizing of his time, particularly on the development and modification of organic forms. He could hardly have missed the pre-Darwinian evolutionary theory current in his day. As his son informs us: "In 1835 Lyell's book on Geology came out and was read by Emerson, in which the ideas of Lamarck, first announced in 1800, were mentioned. . . . These doctrines of Variation in animals through environment and 'effort,' and the transmission of these peculiarities, were at first ridiculed or neglected, but are now recognized as equally necessary in Evolution with Darwin's Natural Selection. Darwin's *Origin of Species* was not published until 1859." [49]

It is unlikely, however, that Emerson's esthetics would have been appreciably different if he had not been exposed to Lamarck's "laws," for his specific applications of Lamarck's organic principles to his own theory of art were singularly meager and incomplete. Indeed, the chief significance of his exposure to the Lamarckian interpretation of development among or-

ganic forms appears to have lain in its preparing him
to accept such specific applications to artistic theory as
were made from similar premises by his friend the
American sculptor and architect Horatio Greenough.

For Emerson's failure to apply the Lamarckian conception of organic development to his theory of art—
at least so far as one might have hoped—two reasons at
once suggest themselves. The first is the inherent im-
practicality of trying, in modern times, to take all
knowledge as one's province, as Emerson did. Emerson's thought, as all students of him well know, is an
excellent place from which to begin thinking in a number of directions; but it is a confusing place to end.
Emerson's mind, owing to the vast range of its attention, is a storehouse of raw materials in the form of
suggestions, but it contains very little of that finished
or near-finished product, the ordered conclusion.

The second reason is that Emerson's friend Greenough had already published, in 1843, a paper on architecture which made the application to esthetic theory
of pre-Darwinian "natural principle" that Emerson had
been contemplating. Emerson, recognizing the validity
of Greenough's application, apparently saw no reason
for repeating the sculptor's performance. He was content to cite Greenough's specific applications as confirmation of his own more general conviction.

Emerson was content, finally, to leave to Greenough
the phrasing of "this law of [artistic] creation" [50] which
he felt so important to the revival of art, because Emerson's concern as an esthetic protestant was not confined

exclusively to art, nor to the creation of beauty in art, but included the artist, the creator—the genius,—as well. Greenough was to Emerson's mind something of a genius and hence worthy to declare that law of artistic creation which Emerson had sensed but not voiced. Having found Greenough in the act of proclaiming a law of artistic creation (and this to his complete satisfaction), Emerson felt more inclined to celebrate the pronouncements of that genius (as he did in his *English Traits*) than to grieve over not having made the pronouncements himself.

5. THE GENIUS AND THE BELIEVER

It is worth noting at this point that Emerson's attitude toward the "genius," in regard to art and intellect, was substantially the equivalent of his attitude toward the "believer," in regard to religion. This is to say that the individual genius figured as the champion of Emerson's esthetic protest in very much the sense that the individual believer figured as the champion of his religious protest; for, to Emerson's mind, genius made the individual the peer of the esthetic institution just as belief made the pietist the peer of the religious institution. Genius, like pietistic faith, connected the individual directly with the divine mind.

In order to understand this connection fully it is necessary to recognize that Emerson's use of the term *genius* suggests that he entertained with regard to it what amounts to a threefold conception. First of all, he conceived of genius as he did of nature, art, and beauty: namely, as an aspect of the divine mind. He asserted accordingly that nature, being the work of the divine mind, was also in effect "the work of genius." [51] Secondly, he conceived of genius as an aspect of the human mind by which it relates to its prototype which is the divine mind. He conceived of genius as a character of human thought, as a "style and act of . . . mind." [52] Finally, he conceived of genius as pertaining to and identified with the individual. This is to say that Emerson saw *the genius* as the individual whose mind possessed, for one reason or another, a style of thought and action directly in accord with that of the divine mind; the individual genius partook, albeit from a distance, of divine genius and reflected accordingly the wisdom of the divine mind. The pronouncements of genius, Emerson considered to be as invincible as those of the prophet-believer. "Genius loves truth, and clings to it," he said. "They [i.e., those who recognized genius in the past] called Ideas Gods, and worshipped intellect. They dared not contravene with knacks and talents the divinity which they recognized in genius." [53]

Since Emerson appears to have envisioned the salvation of art in his day largely in terms of the individual genius, and in view of that genius's connection with the larger, essentially deific aspect of genius, it is worth while to note further the degree to which Emerson outlined the character of his conception. To his way of thinking, genius—both on the level of the divine mind and on that of the human intellect—had two major characteristics, one involving independent thought, the other, creative action.

He had begun to think upon this first aspect of genius, as independent thought, at a relatively early age. He had concluded initially, however, that "genius seems to consist merely in trueness of sight, in using such words as show that the man was an eye-witness, and not a repeater of what was told." [54] But he came eventually to see that the character of independent thought—i.e., of genius—required more than trueness of sight merely, since the virtuoso, the copyist, also possesses that character to a high degree. He concluded, in fact, that genius meant not only independent observation, but also reflective thought ordered imaginatively under the principles (of unity) which govern the operations of nature and the human mind. "The term 'genius,'" Emerson observed, "when used with emphasis, implies imagination; use of symbols, figurative speech. A deep insight will always, like Nature, ultimate its thought in a thing. As soon as a man masters a principle and sees his facts in relation to it, fields, waters, skies, offer to clothe his thoughts in images. Then all men understand him. . . . For he can now find symbols of universal significance, which are readily rendered into any dialect; as a painter, a sculptor, a musician, can in their several ways express the same sentiment of anger, or love, or religion." [55]

These faculties of genius (of knowledge, of observation, and of reflection in terms of principle), said Emerson, "are to be tasked to solve the secret enigmas of science by whose successive development the history of Nature is to be explained." [56] The first function of genius as independent thought was, to Emerson's mind, that of apprehending and formulating the law or laws of natural creation. This, as has been suggested, had been or was being accomplished in Emerson's day by numerous scientific investigators and theorists working in the biological sciences: genius in its primary aspect had already triumphed measurably in Emerson's time. But in its secondary, or from Emerson's point of view its more advanced, aspect, genius had yet to prove itself. The law of creation had as yet to be applied consciously to creative activity, and more specifically to art.

To Emerson, the independent thinker was but half a genius. Not only independent thought, but also creative activity, he said, "is always the style and act of these minds." The style and act of the divine mind, Emerson saw to be plainly that of creation; and that of man's mind, if it were to be worthy of him and his Creator, must be the same. Neoclassic art was at best the product of talent and was to be distinguished at all times from the product of genius. "The difference between Talent and Genius," said Emerson, "is, that Talent says things which he has never heard but once, and Genius things which he has never heard. Genius is power; Talent is applicability," [57] which is to say that talent imitates, however selectively, whereas genius initiates.

It was exclusively by way of this initiative or creative activity that Emerson saw the mind of the artist approach the mind of God. It was only in creating new forms, and new conceptions, that the mind of man might parallel, or perhaps even participate in, the divine mind. "The analogy is always perfect between virtue and genius," he said. "One is ethical, the other intellectual creation. *To create, to create is the proof of a divine presence. Whoever creates is God, and whatever talents are, if the man create not, the pure efflux of Deity is not his.*" [58] It was only thus, by admitting genius unto the creation of art forms, thought Emerson, that man's art might be elevated to the level of nature's, that the artist might achieve that happy hour in which "nature appears . . . one with art" because both nature's and man's art are "the work of genius." [59]

But since, to Emerson's mind, genius was so directly opposed to talent, since the idea of creative activity existed in his mind as the exact antithesis of that which was imitative, it was unlikely that he should find evidence of genius in the derivative art of his day. He himself admitted: "It is in vain that we look for genius to reiterate its miracles in the old arts; it is its instinct to find beauty and holiness in new and necessary fact, in the field and road-side, in the shop and mill. Proceeding from a religious heart it will raise to a divine use the railroad, the insurance office, the joint-stock company." [60] He even went so far as to deny the current validity of those great and ancient plastic arts which had provided much of the impetus to the neoclassical movement. "Already," he said in his essay on art, "History is old enough to witness the old age and disappearance of particular arts. The art of sculpture is long ago perished to any real effect. It was originally a useful art, a mode of writing, a savage's record of gratitude or devotion. . . . But it is the game of a rude and youthful people. . . . In the works of our plastic arts and especially of sculpture, creation is driven into a corner." [61]

Being primarily a poet and essayist and concerned chiefly with the verbal arts, Emerson was capable of observing without qualm that "the office of painting and sculpture seems to be merely initial." [62] And so far as the word-symbol serves not only purposes of artistic expression, but those of communication as well—so far as it is more convenient to think in terms of words than, for example, in terms of statues,—Emerson was absolutely right. Yet when the processes of communication are focused upon such an abstract entity as art, when there exists a most pressing need for specific examples, those plastic and graphic arts which Emerson was wont to dismiss so hastily come again to the fore. No matter how one argues the matter, the fact remains that the work of the sculptor, however abstract, is less removed from those physical aspects which we choose to call reality than is the work of the poet. It is for this very reason, undoubtedly, that Emerson found the first and perhaps strongest confirmations of his own organic esthetic faith expressed most eloquently, not from the lips of either the fieldhand or the roadside millwright (who are, for the most part, un-concerned with "art"), or even from those of the poet, but paradoxically from those of a practitioner of what Emerson had supposed to be the dead and literal art of sculpture.

CHAPTER THREE

1. EMERSON AND GREENOUGH

Horatio Greenough (1805–1852), the most eloquent spokesman of Emerson's esthetic faith, was by trade a portrait sculptor. He did portrait busts of such eminent persons as Lafayette, John Quincy Adams, and James Fenimore Cooper, and his studio in Florence was much visited by Americans abroad. On commission from Congress he produced a massive half-draped statue of Washington which was to have been "enthroned beneath the vaulted arch of the Capitol and gilded by the filtered rays of far-falling sunlight." [1] The statue, being too heavy for the floor supports beneath it and too offensive in its seminudity for the sensibilities of the constituency, was finally set aside to weather upon the grounds outside the Capitol. In style it was, as Professor Matthiessen has said, "a virtually unsurpassable example of derivative neo-classicism." [2] A second colossal piece, a group entitled "The Rescue," also commissioned by Congress, and designed to grace one of the "two buttresses which project from the portico on either side of the main stairway of the Capitol," [3] bore almost exactly the quality in sculpture which in literature is characterized by the novels of Greenough's friend and sponsor James Fenimore Cooper.[4] It included a struggling Indian, a settler, his wife and child, and (considering the activity characterized by the piece) a remarkably placid dog. The group, as Greenough's most sympathetic critic, Tuckerman,[5] has suggested, represented at least moderate daring for Greenough's time, since the figures were not dressed as Greeks and were engaged actively or passively in the exclusively American employment of subduing an Indian.

Greenough's significance as a sculptor is limited primarily to a few relatively insignificant facts: he was "the first American deliberately choosing sculpture as a profession, and going abroad for serious study, he gave the art an importance in the eyes of his countrymen which it never had before";[6] his "'Washington' was the first colossal marble carved by an American, 'The Rescue,' the second." [7] Greenough cannot, on these grounds, be considered to have approached the level of Emerson's "genius" at all, for, as Lorado Taft has suggested, in all fairness (and even as Greenough himself would have admitted), "Greenough produced nothing that might not have been done, better or worse, but in exactly the same spirit, by any sculptor of whatsoever nationality then living in Italy." [8]

It is true that Greenough, like every other practitioner of the arts, however imitative, did in a sense create new forms. However, he did so not according to Emerson's natural law, but rather according to the traditions of ancient Greece, of Rome, and of Florence in his day; and whatever correspondence with nature happened to appear in the style of his art may be considered to have descended circuitously by way of Greek, Roman, and Florentine sculptural traditions. Even in portrait sculpture, at which he appears to have been skillful, Greenough was at best only imitating natural form and not emulating the generative processes of nature—not, at any rate, according to Emerson's way of thinking. It was not Greenough's activity as a sculptor which qualified him in Emerson's estimation as a genius; rather it was the independent character of Greenough's thought. And independent thought, as both Greenough and Emerson were well aware, must invariably precede truly creative activity.

It is perhaps asking too much of the short life of Greenough's genius that it should have succeeded not only in framing an organic "law" of artistic creation but also in putting that law into practice. Indeed, it must be taken into account that all, or nearly all, of Greenough's artistic training was in the very tradition which later he was eloquently to denounce. In order to excuse the gap between his esthetic preachment and his artistic practice, one needs only to recognize that his departure from the neoclassic tradition in art was of appreciably the same radical kind as Emerson's self-separation from the clergy. Greenough lived only a little more than half as long as Emerson. He appears to have come upon his theory late in his life. He lacked time, actually, to put it into action. As Emerson wrote to Carlyle: "Horatio Greenough, a sculptor, but whose tongue was far cunninger in talk than his chisel to carve, and who inspired great hopes, died . . . at forty-seven years." [9]

Greenough's esthetic theory appears to have resulted from continued and growing dissatisfaction with the medium of his own art. It is not entirely by accident that it concerns the architect's art rather than the sculptor's. If the public's rejection of his colossal, neoclassical "Washington" had not given him pause to consider its justification as art, then certainly the new awareness of the laws of creation, or rather of adaptation, among organic forms, as voiced by Lamarck and others, must have borne in upon him the deficiencies of his own endeavors. Although he did not abandon his trade as a sculptor, it is significant that he appears at least to have stopped thinking about it exclusively by the year 1840.

Having learned his trade, Greenough (like Emerson the minister) was not content to remain complacently at the level of operative professional competence. Like Emerson, he was possessed of an inquiring mind and could not, therefore, avoid looking into the vast areas of esthetic speculation wherein his own particular craft took up but one small province. It was from the farther reaches that he assembled those esthetic principles and preachments which together form his qualifications as an esthetic philosopher, a seer, a prophet, and a genius.

Where and how Greenough arrived at those organic esthetic conceptions which he announced, to Emerson's great rejoicing, with such clarity and eloquence— whether he derived them directly from the natural sciences of his day, or from his reading in Emerson or others among the transcendental thinkers, or derived them as a result of his exposure to similarly "transcendental" trends of thought then current in Europe, —may never be known for certain. Whatever the precise "origins" of Greenough's esthetic, the important thing is that his announcement of it was both early and clear, and may well have been the product of truly original thought.

It is also important that although the scope of Greenough's esthetic is vast almost to the degree of universality, it remains focused, nonetheless, upon the art of the builder. Since Greenough had been commissioned late in his life to contribute to the embellishment of the Capitol, there is some suggestion that his esthetic might even have developed out of the turning of his attention to these problems of the artist as builder. But whether he derived his esthetic as a result of an awakened interest in architecture, or whether he derived it independently and then applied it to that art (and it is likely that both these things happened more or less concurrently), Greenough not only apprehended the new, vigorous, organic esthetic, but also saw in the architectural art a better chance of its being realized than in his own art of sculpture.

Emerson himself appears to have recognized the greater readiness with which architecture may be adapted to the organic esthetic than any other of the arts. "There is a closer relation than is commonly thought between the fine arts and the useful arts," he said in his lecture on Michelangelo, adding, "Architecture is the bond that unites the elegant and the economical arts," [10] which is to say in effect that architecture comes closer to unifying the useful with the beautiful (as, for example, it is presumed to be united in nature) than either poetry or sculpture.

It is significant that apart from their tenure of complementary, if not identical, esthetic convictions, the chief bond uniting Emerson and Greenough is their common interest in architecture. It is quite likely that had it not been so, they might not have become such good friends as they did; for apart from this common interest, each had tended to reject the art of the other. Emerson, it will be remembered, had asserted that mankind had developed beyond any use for the primitive art of the sculptor; whereas Greenough, for his part, voiced the sculptor's fear and distrust of the scholarly man of letters, as follows: "We who cut stone temper our tools and choose our blocks by rules that be not in the Encyclopedia or Conversation Lexicon. We are jealous of these knowledges, many of them are vague, dim, guess-work to appearance. When the book-maker doth cross-question us to extract the kernel of our toil, we hang the lip and look silly; under the garb of inarticulate stupidity lies a grim determination that the idler enter not into our rest." [11]

Both Emerson and Greenough appear to have turned to the architectural art, and to have met subsequently upon the ground of that common interest, as a result of their separate dissatisfactions with the nature of their own arts. Inspired as they must have been by their realizations of the vast potential inherent in an organic esthetic, each had run directly upon the disappointing realization that his own art, as it existed in his day, did not apply itself readily to any truly significant illustration of his new esthetic insight.

But if Emerson and Greenough were similarly dissatisfied with the character of their own arts, they were so for nearly opposite reasons. The art of the sculptor, Greenough discovered, was too much limited in its functions or applications to lend itself to the new esthetic; for although sculpture had reached a high level of technical development even in the time of the Greeks and Romans in whose tradition Greenough carved, although the skills appertaining to the art are numerous and not easily mastered, and although the sculptured forms of imitative art may well be extended in variation and increased in number almost infinitely, the applications of sculpture are almost exclusively those of embellishment. The function of the statue is most obviously that of being a statue, an ornament; and beyond that, in Greenough's time, it was seldom anything more. The conscious application of sculptural talents to the problems of design with respect to useful objects was, as yet, far beyond the advanced esthetic conception even of Greenough. Yet in speaking of form in terms of function it is almost necessary that one refer to an art which serves a number of different functions rather than one exclusively; and architecture is just such an art. Greenough turned, because he had to, from sculpture to architecture in search of adequate illustration for his esthetic theory.

Emerson turned from poetry to architecture for a quite different reason. Language, unlike sculpture, has a multitude of functions; and the discernment and isolation of these functions was one of Emerson's chief preoccupations. Emerson's organic conception of beauty and art had led him, as Professor Matthiessen's chapter on "The Organic Principle" suggests, to a consideration of the structure, the growth, the origin and function of language—a consideration which since Emerson's time has inspired such studies of language and of meaning as have resulted in the creation of whole "sciences" such as etymology, symbolic logic, and semantics. In short, Emerson's intellectual curiosity led him to dip into black pools of inquiry which were plainly too deep for wading. As a consequence, Emerson can be seen to have initiated an investigation of the relationships between the forms and functions of language which he

was unequipped to carry out to any significant conclusion. Because he was uncertain of the exact nature
of language, and hence of the character of his art,
Emerson ran into difficulties in trying to explain his
esthetic in terms of his own practice. The "concrete"
materials of his art, being words, were hardly less
abstract than the theories which such materials were
intended to illustrate. For this reason, among others,
Emerson was constantly on the lookout for specific
examples from other, less abstract, arts which might aid
him in illustrating significant aspects of his esthetic
faith.

Like Greenough, he found sculpture unsuited to
the illustration of his theory, and he appears to have
rejected painting on essentially the same grounds. In
architecture, however, he found an art bearing the
physical substance of sculpture or painting, yet with
a variety of functions which approached even that of
language. But Emerson—as Professor Matthiessen's
chapters on him make clear—did not turn as completely away from language in seeking to illustrate his
theory as Greenough did from sculpture; he was aware
that his references to architecture were but substitutes
for the real illustrations (to be taken from language)
which an understanding of his art demanded.

Greenough could turn his attention almost entirely
from sculpture to architecture because he was merely
progressing from a small problem to its larger extension.
Emerson, on the other hand, must have felt compelled
to return always from his incidental references to

architecture and to grapple once more with that vast problem of language which, if solved, might provide the key to a multitude of lesser problems. As a consequence, Emerson's references to architecture remain limited, casual, and scattered. Yet, sketchy as they are, they do suggest a certain order of development in his thinking.

2. EMERSON ON ARCHITECTURE

In Milan, at the age of thirty, looking not at American imitations of Renaissance architecture, but at the "originals," Emerson had noted: "Architecture—shall I speak what I think?—seems to me ever an imitation." [12] "I would rather know," he said, "the metaphysics of architecture, as of shells and flowers, than anything else in the matter." [13] Emerson's subsequent references to the snow cornice as the model of the architectural scroll, to the woodland glade as the model of the Gothic nave, and the like, all suggest an endeavor on his part to apprehend that metaphysics by means of a literal comparison of the forms of man's architecture with those of God's architecture. That Emerson progressed beyond this level of comparison to an awareness of the operation of principle in art, even as in nature, is shown by his reference to the architecture of the Vatican in his essay on "Art." "The traveller," he said, "who visits the Vatican and passes from chamber to chamber through galleries of statues, vases, sarcophagi and candelabra, through all forms of beauty cut in the richest materials, is in danger of forgetting the simplicity of the principles out of which they all sprung, and that they had their origin from thoughts and laws in his own breast." [14]

The very fact, however, that the visitor was in danger of forgetting this was to Emerson's mind a measure of the deficiency of those multifarious "forms of beauty." They were undoubtedly the product of those principles which govern not only nature but also the human mind; but these principles in their operations were disguised, to Emerson's way of thinking, by an unnatural superfluity of forms. Renaissance architecture, to Emerson's mind, lacked the characteristics of economy, of unity, concurrent with diverse abundance, which he held to be characteristic of nature.

This dissatisfaction with the monumental architectures of Europe prepared Emerson admirably for his meeting with Greenough. By the time he met Greenough, he was certain that some significant principle or set of principles underlay the architectural art, indeed all art; but he was not entirely certain of the phrasing. He was convinced that a true announcement of the law of artistic creation in architecture, in all art, was in order—was, in fact, long overdue. He must have been gratified to have discovered in Florence a man who was capable of making, who had actually made already, that announcement—particularly since that man was an American.

Speaking of Greenough and his "theory of structure," Emerson noted in his *English Traits:* "At Florence, chief among artists I found Horatio Greenough, the American sculptor. . . . His paper on Architecture, published in 1843, announced in advance the leading thoughts of Mr. Ruskin on the *morality* in architecture, notwithstanding the antagonism in their views of the history of art. I have a private letter from him,—later, but respecting the same period,—in which he roughly sketches his own theory. 'Here is my theory of structure: A scientific arrangement of spaces and forms to functions and to site; an emphasis of features proportioned to their *gradated* importance in function; color and ornament to be decided and arranged and varied by strictly organic laws, having a distinct reason for each decision; the entire and immediate banishment of all make-shift and make-believe.' " [15] He referred similarly, in *The Conduct of Life*, to one "Möller," presumably the German *Baumeister* Georg Moller (1784–1852), who in an essay on architecture made a similar declaration of the virtue of economy, of dynamic, of organic unity in art.[16] But Emerson's chief enthusiasm was for Greenough, who had worked out his theory at greater length.

Emerson's enthusiastic acceptance of Greenough's esthetic appears to have derived generally from the fact that Greenough, while possessing the same esthetic convictions as Emerson, was better equipped by the technical nature of his prior training to arrive, as Professor Matthiessen has remarked, at "ordered conclusions beyond Emerson's scope" [17]—and thus, to confirm Emerson's faith and advance his protestant argument not only in regard to architecture, but in regard to art generally. However, having accepted Greenough's pronouncements with an enthusiasm which seems to have caused Henry Thoreau to become irrationally hostile toward the sculptor,[18] Emerson returned to the problems of language connected with his own art.

Greenough's pronouncement of the organic or transcendental esthetic was superior to Emerson's not only because Greenough had a surer grasp of the technical details of the plastic arts, but also because, being more an artist and less a religious thinker than Emerson, he was not so heavily burdened in his thinking by the vast load of Plotinian-Christian philosophy which weighted Emerson's every thought. Greenough was not, like Emerson, concerned particularly with the nature of reality, of language, of thought, or of the mind. In taking art alone as his province, he got to know it more intimately than Emerson knew the universe. And knowing it more intimately, he was able to speak of it more clearly than Emerson could.

CHAPTER
FOUR

1. ESTHETICS AT WASHINGTON

Much of what Greenough had to say of art and beauty generally, and of architecture in particular, he collected in a single volume, *The Travels, Observations, and Experience of a Yankee Stonecutter,*[1] published in 1852, the last year of his life. Four of its chapters, namely, "Aesthetics at Washington," "Remarks on American Art," "American Architecture," and "Relative and Independent Beauty," present "clear, clean and civil"[2] statements of Greenough's attitudes toward art and beauty. These four chapters, or essays, and four others not appearing in Greenough's *Travels* but included in an edition of his writings by Henry T. Tuckerman,[3] namely, "Burke on the Beautiful," "Crit-

icism in Search of Beauty," "Structure and Organization," and "Fashion in Relation to Progress," serve
today as the most imposing monuments to his genius.
Taken together, these essays constitute the body of
Greenough's esthetic, an esthetic ordered by such
penetrating insight into the fundamental problems involved in the creation of art, and characterized by such
validity, by such freshness, that its several portions
have recently been collected and reprinted,[4] nearly a
century after their first appearance between covers,
for the reason that "Greenough reads, in the main,
like a progressive contemporary." [5]

Greenough's esthetic appears upon examination to
possess three major aspects, the protestant, the metaphysical, and the prophetic. Each is essentially religious
in tone, and each corresponds more or less exactly to
a similar aspect of Emerson's transcendental esthetic.
That an American sculptor who spent a good half of
his life in Europe should have approached the problem
of art from the same direction as one of the Boston
ministry appears strange at first, but only so long as one
ignores the profound influences of early environment
and training upon the emergent personality. Greenough
was, in fact, as much a product of Boston and Harvard
as Emerson. Like Emerson he was born in Boston (two
and a half years after the poet), and like him he attended Harvard, where he was exposed during his
formative years to very nearly the same intellectual
atmosphere which enveloped Emerson. Although he
was certain from a very early age that he wanted to

[81]

become an artist, Greenough could not, however secular his interests, have escaped being influenced one way or another by the protestant religious traditions which loaded the very atmosphere of Harvard college life.

Indeed, on the basis of his esthetic philosophy as proclaimed in his essays,[6] it was Greenough's early environment and training, certainly, which provided the source, if not even the substance,[7] of his attitude toward art and beauty. His many years in the study and practice of his art abroad, at first in Rome and after that in Florence, appear to have been superimposed, merely, upon that body of New England doctrine from which his esthetic conviction, like Emerson's, stemmed.

As an esthetic protestant, as a critic, Greenough's European training served both for and against him. As a critic, it commanded for him such attention and respect as generally adhere to recognized practitioners of the arts. Anyone who doubted that Greenough knew whereof he spoke with regard to beauty and art had only to look at his works commissioned by Congress for evidence of his recognition as an artist. Yet it was that very work, as nearly every one of Greenough's critics has pointed out, which tended to disguise the true nature of Greenough's esthetic argument, and to nullify it once it was perceived. The most imposing pieces of Greenough's sculpture were plainly neoclassical in form, and he was left ever on that account to explain the gap between his theory and his own practice.

Actually, Greenough, despite the neoclassical styling of his sculpture, was no more a partisan of neoclassical tradition than Emerson. It must be remembered that Greenough was primarily a portrait sculptor and that he had been commissioned to do those two colossal pieces ("Washington" and "The Rescue"), by means of which he is most often damned, as adornment for a building which others had already designed. He is hardly to be censured for designing neoclassical sculpture as embellishment for neoclassical architecture already extant. The true likenesses and differences between Emerson and Greenough are to be sought and found, therefore, less in comparison of Greenough's statuary with Emerson's theory than in comparison of the theories and the lives of these two men taken entire.

As we have remarked, the chief differences in attitude between Emerson and Greenough derive from the fact that Greenough was more an artist and less a religious philosopher than Emerson. Nevertheless, those differences remain—like the differences between Emerson and, for example, Channing—more nearly differences in degree than in substance. Greenough's religious faith, as will be seen, was in essence the same as Emerson's. Indeed, even the difference in emphasis between Greenough's ideas and Emerson's was due chiefly to an element of timing. This is to say, merely, that

Greenough learned earlier in his life than Emerson that he wanted to become an artist. When Greenough went to Europe for the first time in 1825, he knew exactly why he was going; Emerson was not so sure; Emerson continued to preach, intermittently, during the years after his return from Europe in 1833 and did not actually publish his essay on "Nature" until 1836.

Greenough, on the other hand, did not really begin to apprehend the true nature of his calling as an esthetic protestant—as a metaphysician and prophet—until his brief return to America in 1842–1843. Even then, he had been disposed at first to exert only an "indirect and gentle influence within his own sphere." He wrote from Washington to his brother Henry Greenough, December 1, 1842: "The great material interests absorb the country (as is natural), and the most proper thing for an artist here to do is to keep quiet and exert an indirect and gentle influence within his own sphere." [8]

Greenough was unable, however, to remain either quiet or gentle for very long and by 1843 had come forth with a "paper on architecture" [9] in which he denounced American esthetic conception, symbolized by the architecture of Washington and New York, as the worst sort of makeshift—as totally beneath the esthetic potential, beneath even the current needs, of the new nation.

By the time of his death in 1852, Greenough had become evangelically protestant against the neoclassical esthetic traditions instituted by the founding fathers. In his last year he published his *Travels* and was engaged in giving a series of lectures on art. Apparently he no longer felt, as he had felt once, that he could afford to exert a gentle influence only, and this within the limits of his particular artistic field. He had been seized by a compulsion to speak of art not gently, but at full voice, and to all Americans. He was compelled to speak of art, nay even to preach on it, he said, "because I think I see that it is a want—a want widely felt, deeply felt—an intellectual want, a social want, an economical want—and that to a degree which few seem to suspect. I believe that these States need art as a visible exponent of their civilization. They call for it as a salvation from merely material luxury and sensual enjoyment, they require it as the guide and ornament of inevitable structure and manufacture." [10]

What Greenough had to say, finally, about art and architecture amounted to nothing less than a declaration of esthetic independence for American art and for the American artist. The effect of his argument, like that of Emerson's, was to secure for the individual conscience the same rights, within the provinces of art and beauty, which (in America) that conscience was reputed to enjoy already in the realms of religion and polity. Its effect was to complete the emancipation of the protestant individual, to secure his right as judge not only in religion and in polity but also in art, by introducing the genius as the esthetic counterpart of the religious believer and of the politically "natural" man.

The framing of the declaration was no minor under-taking. However, Greenough was aided in that task, as was Emerson, by the availability of such argument developing from the emergent biological sciences as enabled him to back his assertion of independence with a conception of artistic creation fully as powerful and as useful to his particular protestant purpose as those earlier conceptions, of universal priesthood and original virtue, which had been useful to dissenters in religion and politics.

It is true that Greenough's esthetic protest was in nearly all respects the image of Emerson's. But it was that image magnified, and it appeared, wherever it was in focus, more forcefully clear than Emerson's. It is more than likely that both Emerson's and Greenough's protests against the low condition of American art were precipitated by their European experiences. From Europe they had both been able to look back upon American art and see it more clearly than the few Americans at home who were aware that an American art existed. Probably Greenough's protest was more violent than Emerson's for the reason that Greenough, having spent much more time in Europe than Emerson, was less familiar with American art and consequently less indulgent toward it.[11]

Furthermore, Greenough, being a sculptor, was by the very nature of his training more conversant than Emerson with those plastic arts of a country which generally impress themselves first upon the visitor and upon the returning citizen alike. And being concerned primarily with plastic art, rather than with poetry, Greenough could not possibly ignore those distressing deficiencies in his own art which were everywhere in evidence before him. Greenough might conceivably have returned to America without becoming immediately aware of the deficiencies of its literary arts, which reside, after all, in books primarily;[12] but he could not, being in Washington, avoid observing the enormities of American architecture.

Recognizing in that architecture the condition of American esthetics generally, Greenough could not, as a loyal citizen, remain silent. He found it necessary to speak, to protest, to criticize, both in the interest of such high art as America deserved, and in opposition to such art as he could see around him. Greenough, in speaking of American art, took that art which was most immediately apparent to him in the nation's capital as the product, the symbol, of American esthetics in general. It was natural that his attention should have become so focused; it was to Washington, after all, that he had returned in 1843 and 1851 in pursuance of work commissioned by Congress, and it was there that he might reasonably have expected to find assembled the noblest productions of American craft and genius, particularly in the plastic and graphic arts. But there was little in Washington that Greenough could honestly commend, and much that he felt compelled to condemn.

[87]

2. CRITICISM IN WASHINGTON

Greenough complained that statuary was placed, more often than not, without mature attention to its surroundings. He complained of the selection of site for Persico's group, "Columbus and the Indian Girl," [13] as "anomalous and absurd; anomalous because it invades the front view of the portico [of the Capitol], chokes the façade, and hides another statue by the same artist; absurd, because it treats the building as somewhat on which to mount into conspicuous view, not as a noble and important vase which it is called humbly to adorn and illustrate." [14] He complained that his own "Washington," which had been set up out-of-doors, was surrounded by dwarf cypress and clumps of rosebush. "These," he said, "are impertinent and ridiculous— impertinent because they hide the pedestal and obstruct the view of the inscription, thus overlaying the intention of the monument, and that for the mere display of ephemeral vegetation, a phenomenon, however attractive, not here in place—ridiculous, because they seem as if intended in some way to help and eke out the sculpture; which, when a statue of this class requires it, must be done by replacing it with something worthy to stand alone." [15]

He protested that sculpture, if it be of any value, should not be exposed to needless damage: "I have several times seen boys at play on the portico of the Capitol; which, if right, makes it wrong there to place costly sculptures." [16] Nor did he accept with any kindness the concession of putting up protective railings. "If I protest against iron railings about statuary," he said, "it is because I believe they avail not for their object. I trust to the intelligence of the many to do justice to the artistic efforts made for their sake." [17] Just in case, however, Greenough would have preferred to see statuary so placed as to discourage climbing on it. Even worse, perhaps, than inattention to the correct placing or proper maintenance of sculpture was attention ill advised. "Four lamps," he observed, "have been placed around the statue of Washington; by night they light only the feet of the figure, by day they exactly obstruct two of the principal views of it. I doubt not that the person who so placed these lights meant to do the statue a service. He probably never heard of 'the eight views' of a statue." [18]

But the esthetic enormities perpetrated in bumbling good faith against sculptures by artists like Persico and himself were nothing, in Greenough's eyes, as compared with that single monstrosity, already rising, which was to represent the entire nation as its memorial tribute to George Washington. No amount of shrubbery could ever have hidden its vast inconsistencies. If completed as originally planned, it would have been less a memorial to Washington than a monument to the confused state of American esthetics.

The design pictured "an obelisk rising out of a low circular building whose exterior presents a Greek colonnade of the Doric order . . . the intermarriage of an Egyptian monument . . . with a Greek structure, or one of Greek elements. . . . I do not think it is in the power of art," said Greenough, "to effect such an amalgamation without corrupting and destroying the special beauties and characters of the two elements. The one, simple even unto monotony, may be defined as a gigantic expression of unity; the other, a combination of organized parts assembled for a common object. The very perfection of their forms as exponents of so distinct characters makes them protest against juxtaposition. If the union of Egyptian mass and weight with Greek combination and harmony be heterodox, the order in which they are here displayed is even more strikingly a violation of propriety. The complex, subdivided, comparatively light Greek structure is placed as a basis, a foundation. The Egyptian mass of stone rises above it. When this arrangement is stated, I must think that its palpable absurdity is demonstrated. It may be urged that those weaker and more slender columns veil a massive foundation within them. We had guessed this already, because a miracle alone could otherwise sustain the weight. The *pillars* hide the strength of the structure, hence their impertinence as an architectural feature. It is incumbent upon edifices, first, to be strong; secondly, TO LOOK STRONG. We have read of a colossus of brass with feet of clay, and the image is striking. To an architect, Egyptian weight sustained in appearance by Greek pillars is not less so." [19]

For his own part, Greenough would have chosen the form of an obelisk unadorned, and of very nearly the proportions but not the magnitude of the present Washington monument. "The obelisk," he said, "has to my eye a singular aptitude, in its form and character, to call attention to a spot memorable in history. It says but one word, but it speaks loud. If I understand its voice, it says, Here! It says no more." [20] However, Greenough would have had that obelisk a "monolith, a single shaft of granite," rather than "five hundred feet of granite built as chimneys are, stone upon stone." [21] "A monolith," he said, "has a value like that of a diamond—a value which increases in a geometric ratio with its weight. Why? Because its extraction from the quarry, its elaboration and safe erection, show not only wealth but *science*." [22]

In concluding his criticism, Greenough observed "that there is scarce an architect in the country that could not have demonstrated the absurdity of the monument I have examined, and have thus prevented its consummation." But "why," he asked, "were they all silent?" [23] This was but one of a number of embarrassing questions which Greenough asked of architects in his day. For it was in architecture, as represented by the public buildings in Washington, that Greenough found the very lowest condition of American art. There he found not only those excessive evidences of ignorance, of inattention, and of inconsistency which characterized the treatment of sculptures and monuments, but also a vast welter of inconvenience, of inefficiency, in the conduct of the public business—all traceable directly to the heedless employment of ancient forms for modern uses. He asked to know why those forms which represented the highest achievement in American public architecture had been allowed to interfere with their very functions.

Greenough asked of American architects some explanation for the more obvious, external, deficiencies of their art. He wanted to know why, for example, the Capitol had been constructed of a local, Potomac stone so soft that it required paint to keep it from washing entirely away; and why, in view of the known deficiencies of the stone, presumably responsible architects had permitted a "deplorable recurrence to the same quarries for the construction of the Patent Office and the Treasury buildings. The outlay in paint alone," he observed, "to which recourse has been had in order to sheathe this friable material, would have maintained a school which would have saved us from the blunder . . . Had the amount expended in white lead been invested, a fund would have now accumulated sufficient to reface them all with marble." [24] "What shall we say," he asked, "of the balustrades, where iron bars have been driven bodily into the columns as though a column in a first-class building might be treated like a blind wall in the basest structure, and that, too, without a shadow of a need? What shall we say of the iron railings that obtrude upon the eye about the blockings of the Patent Office, and veil, with their inharmonious blackness, the organization of that building? What of the one slender chimney of red brick which peers over the broken profile of the marble Post Office? Will any adept in the science of construction explain why the gaslight which is seen at the eastern entrance of the Capitol was made to hang with so many feet of tiny pipe, and then secured by shabby wires driven into the columns?" [25]

More significantly, he wished to learn of American architects why the monumental, or external, aspects of public building in Washington had been allowed to usurp the attention of designers, to the detriment of those internal, those functional, aspects by which architecture serves the occupants of buildings. Of the Capitol itself he wrote: "I have been assured by one of the chief officers of a department that one-half of the employees of his section of the administration were required only by the blundering and ignorant arrangement of the edifice." [26] On the outside, the public architecture had succeeded, however poorly, in imitating at least the grandeur of ancient, and presumably democratic, Greece; but on the inside it had failed in the more important task of providing adequately for the agencies of present democratic government. Greenough sought to know, on this account, exactly why architecture in Washington had so failed the government that sponsored it.

It is unlikely that he expected to hear any adequate answers to the questions he asked from the architects of his own time. If the architects had known the answers—if, even, they had been aware previously of the questions—they very likely would not have made those mistakes which prompted his inquiries. And since those whom he asked were unlikely to answer him adequately, and he was the one, after all, who had raised the issue, it was rather clearly his obligation to answer his own questions. In answering them, in concerning himself not only with what was wrong with American art but also with why it was wrong, Greenough extended the scope of his criticism far beyond mere faultfinding—into the broader realm of critical analysis—and approached, in the process, that high level of esthetic protest upon which Emerson operated.

Like Emerson, Greenough ascribed the low condition of American art to the fact that Americans had never really thought seriously about art and beauty. Of architecture in particular he observed: "The mind of this country has never been seriously applied to the subject of building. Intently engaged in matters of more pressing importance, we have been content to receive our notions of architecture as we have received the fashion of our garments and the form of our entertainments, from Europe. In our eagerness to appropriate, we have neglected to adapt, to distinguish,— nay, to understand. We have built small Gothic temples of wood. . . . Captivated by the classic symmetry of the Athenian models, we have sought to bring the Parthenon into our streets, to make the temple of Theseus work in our towns." [27] As a result, he said, "the Greek temple, as seen among us, claims pity for its degraded majesty, and attests the barbarian force which has abused its nature and been blind to its qualities." [28]

In this respect, Greenough saw in American architecture, even as he had seen in "the architecture of Greece, of Italy, and of the more recent civilizations, . . . a struggle between an indigenous type, born of the soil and of the earlier wants of a people, and an imported theory which, standing upon a higher artistic ground, captivates the eye and wins the approval of dawning taste." [29] And he saw, as a result of this conflict, a confusing "absence of any clear and distinct idea of what is becoming, dignified, and proper," not only in regard to architecture in America, but in regard to art generally. But "for this," Greenough added, "no one is to blame." [30] He perceived the confusion of esthetic judgment in America to be the natural outcome of its history.

The original, the native esthetic tradition in America, Greenough saw clearly as having grown from the conditions of frontier society. This native esthetic, he observed, was negative. "We are still imbued, deeply imbued," he wrote, "with the stern disregard of everything not materially indispensable which was generated by ages of colonial, and border, and semisavage life." [31] It was such an esthetic as one might have expected to find in the American colonies, settled by protestants primarily, and for the purposes originally of making money. Stockholders in the Plymouth and Virginia Companies were more interested in deriving return from their investment than in encouraging the arts in the New World. Nor did the rigors of "border, and semisavage life" encourage the settlers themselves to take to art. Accordingly, and as a consequence of the continuation of frontier society through two hundred years, and as a further consequence of a significant influx into the country, in the middle colonial period, of radical protestants whose tendency it was to deny art altogether, there developed in America a native, strongly utilitarian, predominantly negative esthetic tradition with which Americans even in Greenough's time were "still . . . deeply imbued."

Yet this negative esthetic theory did not extinguish the American citizen's need of esthetic satisfaction. In denying the artist as a member of society, without at the same time inhibiting all demand for art, this native esthetic, in effect, relegated the satisfaction of America's artistic taste to the importer of art from abroad, and thereby focused the attention of a dawning esthetic consciousness not upon native but upon European forms. It led, as Greenough observed, to the acceptance of a derivative esthetic, born of commerce, which for a time almost entirely supplanted the native esthetic.

In an exclusively frontier society, as Greenough willingly admitted, reliance on imported art was perhaps justified. But American society by 1840 was not exclusively a frontier society, nor had it been for some time. By then there existed leisure and security enough to permit the practice of art, and some serious thinking about the problems of art and beauty. Unfortunately, as Greenough observed, the thinking was not being done—not, at least, so far as architecture was concerned—even though many were actively engaged in the production of its forms. The trouble was that America's reliance upon Europe in matters of art and beauty, although no longer justified entirely by frontier conditions, had become traditional.

3. PROTEST IN WASHINGTON

It was against the traditional reliance upon Europe for esthetic guidance that Greenough protested. He saw it leading to the decadence rather than the refinement of esthetic sensitivity in America. Like Emerson, he was aware that although the devices of importation and, subsequently, of imitation had been employed perhaps justifiably in satisfying the esthetic requirements of a semibarbaric, frontier culture, they might never take the place of thought in the creation of a higher art. And like Emerson he was careful, accordingly, to distinguish between an esthetic born of commerce, which displayed wealth primarily, and an esthetic born of thought, which revealed high truth and beauty. "The monuments of Egypt and of Greece," he noted, "are sublime as expressions of their power and their feeling. The modern nation that appropriates them displays only wealth in so doing." [32] For evidence in support of his contention, he needed only to refer again to those examples of the architectural art in America which stood in Washington.

Apparently, however, Greenough had thought at first (upon returning to America) that the low condition of American art—that the American artist's disinclination to think seriously about the nature and

problems of his art—represented a transitory state
merely, an interruption in the native development
toward a mature esthetic consciousness. He was not
much disturbed, therefore, until he became aware that
the reliance upon Europe was increasing, that more
importation and more imitation were the order of the
day. European manufacturers were taking advantage
of the inconsistent American esthetic. "Joyfully," he
observed, "have the governing men of England, France
and Germany beheld in the United States that policy
which has denied all national education except for the
purpose of war and trade. Joyfully have they seen the
individual States equally blind to the swift-coming
requirements of this people; and they have founded
and perfected schools of design, of which the abler
pupils are employed in illustrating the national history
the lower talents fill the factory, the foundry, and the
atelier, to fashion fabrics for ourselves. From Boston to
New Orleans no house, no tavern, no barroom, I had
almost said, that does not give proof, by the tawdry
spawn of European manufacture, of our tribute to their
savoir faire and their appreciation of our taste." [3]
Even local artists, Greenough observed, "have been
compelled," as a result of the great pressure of European influence, "to design and to adorn" in accord with
that influence; and their "efforts, from their nature
must remain monuments of chaotic disorder in all
that relates to esthetics. In a word, we have negative
qualities to deal with before we can rise to zero." [3]
"I do not mean to say," he went on, "that the beautiful

has not been sought and found amongst us. I wish, and I hope to show, that we have done more, in a right direction, than has been appreciated." [35] But he concluded that we had done "much in a wrong direction, that must be examined and repudiated." [36]

Greenough's esthetic protest, like Emerson's, was lodged primarily against the institution rather than the individual. Thus, having observed that "the number and variety of our experiments in building show the dissatisfaction of the public taste with what has been hitherto achieved; the expense at which they have been made proves how strong is the yearning after excellence," and having taken into account "the talents and acquirements of the artists whose services have been engaged," he concluded that the evidence was sufficient "to convince us that the fault lies in the system, not in the men." [37] The "system," of course, was that of the neoclassicist, whose esthetic not only had dominated eighteenth-century Europe, but—enlarging and extending in its application beyond classical antiquity, to the Gothic, to any and all forms of antiquity whatsoever —had extended its dominion well into the nineteenth century. Greenough charged that this "system" led ultimately to the decadence of art; and he was prepared to cite evidence in Europe, as well as in America, to support his charge. No less so than in Washington, or in Boston, he observed, has "the magnificence of the Romans, the splendor of Venice and Genoa, like the ambitious efforts of France, England, and Germany in more recent days, had a certain taint of dilettantism in their origin, which, aiming to combine inconsistent qualities, and that for a comparatively low motive carried through all their happiest combinations the original sin of impotence, and gave, as a result, bombast instead of eloquence, fritter instead of richness, baldness for simplicity, carving in lieu of sculpture." [38]

The decadence of this "system" he saw in terms of two major symptoms, inconsistency and tyranny. Of all the "inconsistencies" which he perceived in examining this system, the most obvious were those temporal-spatial ones which attended the transportation of ancient forms over long distances to the areas of modern culture. Thus the Greek temple in Wall Street, the Roman cathedral in London, revealed themselves clearly as out of time and place. Yet of these more obvious inconsistencies Greenough had relatively little to say; not because he did not perceive them nor because he thought them unimportant, but rather because their presence led him immediately to the contemplation of larger inconsistencies apparent in the relationships between form and function. It was these larger inconsistencies that Greenough considered the chief signs of decadence. "If we trace architecture," he said, "from its perfection in the days of Pericles to its manifest decay in the reign of Constantine, we shall find that one of the surest symptoms of decline was the adoption of admired forms and models for purposes not contemplated in their invention." [39]

Greenough insisted upon looking at art in terms of function as well as of history. And like Emerson, he saw the inconsistencies of the neoclassical, or historical, esthetic revealed even more clearly in architecture than in his own art. The functions of sculpture may be monumental, when it is done in the grand style. The functions of architecture, as Greenough observed, are at least twofold, and monumentality is not the first consideration, but the second. "In all remarks upon important public edifices," he said, "there is a twofold subject under contemplation: first, the organic structure of the works; second, their monumental character." [40]

It was the double function of architecture which pointed up to Greenough the chief deficiencies of the derivative, neoclassic esthetic, revealing it finally, as it appeared in its application to architecture in Washington, reduced very nearly to absurdity. Even when executed with greater skill, and with greater attention to detail, than was exhibited by architects in Washington, that esthetic could not, to Greenough's way of thinking, be applied to architecture—in Washington, or anywhere else for that matter—to any truly great effect. "The laws of expression are such," he said, "that the various combinations which have sought to lodge modern functions in buildings composed of ancient elements, developed and perfected for other objects, betray, in spite of all the skill that has been brought to bear upon them, their bastard origin." [41]

Greenough saw clearly, not only in architecture at Washington, but equally in that at Rome, a major conflict between the organic and the monumental functions of the builder's art. And, as might be expected, when it came to choosing which function should be given priority over the other, Greenough chose the organic; that is, he chose to consider organization before embellishment. "To plant a building firmly on the ground," he said, "to give it the light that may, the air that must, be needed; to apportion the spaces for convenience, decide their size, and model their shapes for their functions—these acts organize a building. No college of architects is a quorum to judge this part of the task. The occupants alone can say if they have been well served; time alone can stamp any building as solid." [42]

In granting priority to the organic over the monumental aspect, Greenough was not, as his detractors might have argued, taking an easy way out. He was not denying the validity of history, of ruins, of ancient architecture *per se,* in order to avoid having to recognize and to deal with the skills embodied in ancient art. He was merely denying that ancient forms could serve the functions of modern society as well as forms derived from a mature consideration of those functions. Indeed, in denying the antiquarian's solution to the problem of providing forms for a changing society, he exposed the artist to even greater problems than those presented by the antiquarian esthetic: he called upon the architect to invent new forms rather than adapt ancient ones. And invention, as he was well aware, involves some of the most rigorous disciplines extant. "To ascertain," he observed, "what the organic requirements of a building like the Capitol are, is in itself a most laborious task. To meet them requires all the science we possess. Have we not seen the House of Lords, in spite of all the experience and the knowledge brought to bear upon the vast outlay that reared it, pronounced a gewgaw by the men who were obliged to work therein? Discomfort and annoyance soon find utterance." [43] The monumental functions of architecture, however carefully attended, count for naught when the organic functions have been neglected. "Decoration and magnificence in such cases," he observed, "like the velvet and gilding of a ship's cabin, seen with seasick eyes, aggravate our discontent." [44]

In giving priority to the organic aspect of architecture, Greenough did not deny the monumental aspect. He did, however, redefine it. "The monumental character of a building," he asserted, "has reference to its site —to its adaptation in size and form to that site. It has reference also to the external expression of the inward functions of the building—to adaptation of its features and their gradation to its dignity and importance." [45] Of the relation of that monumental character to antiquity, however, Greenough had nothing constructive to say.

Greenough's inclination to subordinate the monumental aspects of architecture to the organic aspects appears to have been due at least in part to his adherence to the native American esthetic tradition, which was utilitarian. But it was due also to his protestant background and temperament; for Greenough's reaction against the neoclassical, or derivative, esthetic dominant in his time was founded not only upon his perception of its gross inconsistencies, but also upon his conviction that its hold upon an emergent American art was becoming increasingly powerful—nay, even tyrannical.

Indeed, Greenough's great fear for the future of American art was that it might come under the permanent dominion of an antiquarian esthetic, administered, as in Europe, by a national academy. As an artist, he feared the national academy as much as the radical protestant feared the national church. "We might as well have proposed a national church establishment," he said; and added, "If we look to countries grown old in European systems, it must be for warning rather than for example." [46] America's great esthetic opportunity, to Greenough's mind, lay in the fact that, having been untutored in art and beauty, America had remained relatively free from the European academic system of tutorship in these matters. Error, although rampant in America—if Washington was any measure of conditions throughout the nation,—had not, at any rate, become institutionalized. There was in America no state esthetic, no national academy of art, any more than there was a state church. Indeed, said Greenough, "if Europe must furnish a model of artistic tuition, let us go at once to the records of the great age of art in Italy, and we shall there learn that Michelangelo and Raphael, and their teachers also, were formed without any of the cumbrous machinery and mill-horse discipline of a modern academy. They were instructed, it is true; they were apprenticed to painters. Instead of passively listening to an experienced proficient merely, they discussed with their fellow students the merits of different works, the advantages of rival methods, the choice between contradictory authorities. They formed one another." [47]

Greenough's chief complaint against the academic system was that it placed the student, particularly the genius, in direct competition with his instructor. "In these latter days," he wrote, "classes of boys toil through the rudiments under the eye of men who are themselves aspirants for the public favor, and who, deriving no benefit, as masters of their apprentices, from the proficiency of the lads, look upon every clever graduate as a stumbling-block in their own way. Hence their system of stupefying discipline, their tying down the pupil to mere manual execution, their silence in regard to principles, their cold reception of all attempts to invent." [48] This he called a "routine of instruction which, after years of drudgery and labor, sends forth the genius and the blockhead . . . nearly on a level with each other, the one manacled with precepts, the other armed with them at all points." [49] Accordingly, he saw the academy, the esthetic institution, preëminently as the enemy of genius, its weapon the tyranny of "law." "The president and the professors of an academy," he said, "are regarded by the public as, of course, at the head of their respective professions. Their works are models, their opinions give the law.

The youth are awed and dazzled by their titles and their fame; the man of genius finds them arrayed in solid phalanx to combat his claim." [50] The institution, Greenough was aware, tends to reward its custodians, that is, those who perpetuate, who enforce, and who accept its conventions.

But "the man of genius," as Greenough envisioned him, was, like the protestant believer, not the servant of the institution, but rather the servant exclusively "of a God whose service is perfect freedom." [51] Thus, to Greenough as to Emerson, the genius figured as champion against the tyranny of esthetic institutions; in effect, as the esthetic counterpart of the protestant religious believer. This parallelism in Greenough's mind between the individual genius and the individual protestant believer was reflected, and is shown even more clearly, in his parallel conceptions of academy and church as the chief threats to artistic and religious freedom. In his short essay on "The Smithsonian Institution," he wrote: "I was wandering, the evening of my arrival in Washington, after nine years' absence; musing as I walked, I found myself on the banks of the Potomac. . . . Suddenly . . . the dark form of the Smithsonian palace rose between me and the white Capitol, and I stopped. Tower and battlement, and all that medieval confusion, stamped itself on the halls of Congress, as ink on paper! Dark on that whiteness— complication on that simplicity! It scared me." [52] That shadow suggested to Greenough the shadow of medieval Catholicism upon nations. Temperately he went on: "I have seen the Italian clergy nearly—sometimes intimately,—from the prelate to the begging friar; I have admired their scholars, and have loved their men. I revere the bridge over which our faith has been borne to us. I am not so ignorant of history as to repudiate the sagacious preservers of the old Latin civilization. Still," he added in explanation, "I have brought from that land a fear of their doctrine and a hatred of their politics. I fear their doctrine because it seems to lull and to benumb the general, the average mind, while it rouses and spurs the few. I fear it the more because others do not fear it. I hate their politics because they are hostile to ours. This it was that made me shudder at that dark pile—that castle of authority— that outwork of prescription. . . . There is a certain mystery about those towers and steep belfries that makes me uneasy. . . . Is no *coup d'état* lurking there?" [53]

Thus, in the same sense as Emerson, Greenough was an anarchist; that is, he opposed on general principles the oppressiveness of institutions. Like Emerson, however, he did not extend his opposition to the point of absurdity. "Implicit conformity to precedent obliterates and annihilates the individual," said Greenough; but he added, "violation of it, not justified by theory, or practical result, sets the individual on no enviable pedestal." [54] Far from being opposed to institutions altogether, Greenough was himself the proponent of an esthetic institution: not, however, "a Smithsonian school, with a hierarchy of dignitaries in art," but rather a system of "working normal schools of structure and ornament, organized simply but effectively, and constantly occupied in designing for the manufacturers, and for all mechanics who need aesthetical guidance in their operations—schools where emulation shall be kindled by well-considered stimuli, and where all that is vitally important in building or ornament shall be thoroughly taught and constantly practiced." [55] He even spoke favorably of a school existing in his time at New York: "If there be any youth toiling through the rudiments of art at the forms of the simple and efficient school at New York (whose title is the only pompous thing about it) with a chilling belief that elsewhere the difficulties he struggles with are removed or modified, we call upon him to be of good cheer and to believe— what from our hearts we are convinced of—that there is at present no country where the development and growth of an artist is more free, healthful, and happy than it is in these United States." [56] His complaint against the academic institution lay not exclusively in the fact that it represented art institutionalized, but rather in the fact that the academy, as it was functioning in Europe, and as Greenough feared it might come to function in America, tended to prohibit the exercise of genius except within the narrow limits of an essentially static, neoclassic point of view.

Like Emerson, he elected to bypass the more immediate outworks and sentinels of proscription in order to launch a direct, penetrating attack against the basic premises upon and around which the entire bulwark of neoclassical tradition had been erected. Like Emerson, he saw the neoclassic esthetic to be concerned chiefly with the literal and essentially static unities of balance and of one-to-one correspondence with ancient forms. And assuming, as did Emerson, that the divine mind is wiser than the mind of man—that God's art (nature), in representing the divine mind, must necessarily be superior to that art, however ancient, which represents the mind of man merely,—Greenough could only conclude that the neoclassicist had erred in apprenticing himself to a relatively dull and clumsy association of journeymen. He denied, accordingly, the validity of "taste" advanced in the name of human authority. It is foolish, he asserted, to assume that "the Creator, who formed man's soul with a thirst for sin, and his body as a temple of shame, has [at the same time] made his taste infallible." [57] Like Emerson, Greenough saw in nature a vaster repository of artistic truths, a higher court for taste, than in all of human history; and he counted the esthetician who consulted antiquity and not nature as singularly shortsighted.

In this direction Greenough effectively extended Emerson's main argument, that the neoclassicist's esthetic was not valid so far as it derived from a limited point of view, by advancing the additional argument that the neoclassicist, because his point of view was limited, had formulated his esthetic conception "prematurely." This charge of Greenough's was, to be sure, a paraphrase of Emerson's contention that the neoclassicist had not thought sufficiently on the nature of unity, of beauty, and of art. But Greenough reasoned beyond mere paraphrase to the point of advancing directly an argument which Emerson had not made except by implication, namely, that the neoclassicist's limited point of view had led to the development of a static esthetic conception. This, in view of Emerson's and Greenough's cosmology, was a charge which, if sustained, could deal perhaps a decisive blow against the opposition.

Emerson's and Greenough's conception of the cosmos, it will be remembered, was not static after the manner of eighteenth-century conception, but rather dynamic, or organic. To Greenough, as to Emerson, the cosmos was more faithfully pictured as a growing plant than as a ticking watch. Hence, to Greenough's way of thinking, it was in ignoring the vast flux that is nature—in ignoring the nonstatic, or relative, nature of truth, particularly of esthetic truth—and in accepting prematurely the assessments of a limited, static point of view, that the neoclassicist had erred in framing the tenets of his esthetic. Such tenets could lead only to confusion when applied to a universe in flux. "To deal," said Greenough, "with relative elements as if they were positive is to insure discord and disorganization." [58] When enforced, he added, such tenets could lead only to tyranny. "To assert that this or that form or color is beautiful *per se*," he said, "is to formulate prematurely; it is to arrogate godship; and once that false step is taken, human-godship or tyranny is inevitable without a change of creed." [59]

The result, he asserted, of applying a static esthetic to artistic production—of dealing thus with relative elements as positive, of asserting particular forms and colors to be beautiful *per se*—was such an art as confronted him at Washington, an art characterized by arbitrary, by nondemonstrable embellishment, by false beauty. It was an essentially peripheral art distinguished chiefly by its ornament. And it was so, he argued, because the esthetic conception operating behind it was also peripheral, having failed to expose the heart of the matter with which it was concerned. In short, the deficiencies of that art were the symptoms of a deficient esthetic conception.

Chief of these symptoms, to Greenough's mind, was the use of nondemonstrable, or arbitrary, embellishment borrowed from ancient forms for the service of modern functions alien to them. The result, he observed, was the assertion of "false completeness" in art, the creation of "false beauty." In his essay on "Relative and Independent Beauty" he explains briefly his idea: "I have spoken of embellishment as false beauty. I will briefly develop this view of embellishment. Man is an ideal being; standing, himself inchoate and incomplete, amid the concrete manifestations of nature, his first observation recognizes defect; his first action is an effort to complete his being. Not gifted, as the brutes, with an instinctive sense of completeness, he stands alone as capable of conative action. He studies himself; he disciplines himself. Now, his best efforts at organization falling short of the need that is in his heart, and therefore infinite, he has sought to compensate for the defect in his plan by a charm of execution. Tasting sensuously the effect of a rhythm and harmony in God's world, beyond any adaptation of means to ends that his reason could measure and approve, he has sought to perfect his own approximation of the essential by crowning it with a wreath of measured and musical, yet nondemonstrable adjunct. Now, I affirm that, from the ground whereon I stand and whence I think I see him operate, he thus mirrors, but darkly, God's world. . . . I understand, therefore, by embellishment, THE IN- STINCTIVE EFFORT OF INFANT CIVILIZATION TO DISGUISE ITS INCOMPLETENESS, EVEN AS GOD'S COMPLETENESS IS TO INFANT SCIENCE DISGUISED." [60]

Nondemonstrable, or nonfunctional embellishment, then, represented to Greenough's mind an endeavor on the part of the artist to disguise the inadequacy of his esthetic conception. But so great, asserted Greenough, was the inadequacy, the incompleteness, of the con- ception which dominated art in his time, that it could not be disguised. Hence the restless character of de- rivative art, hence the abandonment of Greek models for Roman, of Roman for Gothic, of Gothic for Palla- dian. "Let us seek," said Greenough, "through the whole history of arbitrary embellishment to find a rest- ing place. We shall look in vain; for the introduction of the inorganic into the organized is destruction; its de- velopment has ever been a *reductio ad absurdum*." [61] Such is the inadequacy of derivative esthetic concep- tion, he argued, that even when dedicated to the highest models—to the forms of nature itself—it effects only the corruption of those forms, rather than the elevation of art: "The leaf, the flower, . . . have, among other similar functional arrangements, been pressed into the service of the decorator to fill that vacuum which the heart of man abhors. The eye responds inevitably to the sensuous charm and the associated expression of these forms; but if we reflect deeply on the source of this gratification we shall detect their real character. Thus enjoyed, this rhythm is never truly generative; for if the organizations they were intended to complete had *no requirement* of their *own,* whose space and means have been *usurped* by their quotations, then I affirm that these extraneous and irrelevant forms invade that *silence* which alone is worthy of a man when there is nothing to be said." [62]

It is not enough, asserted Greenough, to apply literally to art the forms that may be taken from nature—any more than it is enough to employ forms derived from prior arts. Indeed, when natural forms are used as models the deficiencies of a derivative esthetic become even more apparent than when art derives from ancient forms; for even though the artist imitates the highest natural models, his forms issue forth corrupt nonetheless, and thus it becomes most clearly apparent that the trouble lies rather in the artist's static frame of reference than in his models.

To Greenough, as to Emerson, nature provided the highest court of appeal in matters of art and beauty. From nature were to be derived the highest principles of esthetic truth, and in nature were to be found the finest illustrations of that truth. But nature's book was not, to Greenough's mind, a volume to be mastered by the tracing of its illustrations merely. "He who seeks the beautiful in the stupendous system of nature," he said, "will seek in vain for a positive entity whose elements, cognizable by sense, can be set down like the ingredients of a dish or the inventory of a portmanteau." [63]

Indeed, to Greenough, nature must remain misunderstood and art must remain incomplete and hence false so long as the artist continues to consider the creation of beauty primarily in terms of imitative embellishment. That so limited a consideration of beauty was inevitable, even valuable in advancing art along the road toward a mature esthetic, Greenough (like Emerson) did not deny. As in politics, said Greenough, "the monarch rises out of savage manhood . . . so will every development of real humanity [including art] pass through a phase of nondemonstrable embellishment, which is a false completeness." [64] But nondemonstrable embellishment was not, to Greenough's way of thinking, the highest possible condition in art, any more than monarchy was the highest possible condition in politics. To Greenough, therefore, the most important consideration was to keep art in his time from crystallizing in its existing state of false completeness; it was most urgently the duty of the artist, of the esthetician, to prevent that eventuality. And this duty, he observed, committed the artist, the esthetician, to two major tasks.

The first was that of advancing esthetic principle in the direction of that true "completeness [which] is the absolute utterance of the Godhead." [65] The second was that of developing artistic performance until the forms of man's art might approximate, in part at least, "the completeness of the sea . . . ; the completeness of earth, whose every atom is a microcosm; the completeness of the human body, . . ." [66]

It is important to note that the term *completeness,* as used by Greenough, bears a much larger meaning than is usually assigned to it. It refers to a conception which is equivalent both in magnitude and in substance to Emerson's conception of *unity.* The relationship is more than fortuitous; it is due, indeed, to the fact that Greenough's esthetic conception, his esthetic faith, was unitarian in the same essentially religious sense as Emerson's.

4. A UNITARIAN ESTHETIC CONCEPTION

Although Greenough never trained for the ministry, and indeed seems never to have inclined toward any vocation outside the arts, his attitude toward art was not only avowedly religious, but militantly unitarian. For example, he speaks in his essay on "Relative and Independent Beauty" of "seeking, through artistic analysis, a confirmation of my belief in one God." [67] And he argues, in the same essay: "I base my opinion of embellishment upon the hypothesis that there is not one truth in religion, another in mathematics, and a third in physics and in art; but that there is one truth, even as one God, *and that organization is his utterance*." [68]

In appreciably the same sense, then, as Emerson, Greenough concerned himself with apprehending in nature, and with transferring to art, what amounts to a cosmic relationship of unity, of completeness, whereby the work of art, even as the object in nature, stands in valid relationship to all things. Turning to nature, with this objective in mind, he saw there (as had the neoclassicist before him) order—order, however, viewed dynamically, not statically. "I feel justified," he said, "in taking the ground that organization [that order] is the primal law of structure, and I suppose it, even where my imperfect light cannot trace it, unless embellishment can be demonstrated." [69] By way of illustration, Greenough remarked that "the lily is arrayed in heavenly beauty [is connected, in effect, with Deity] because it is organized, both in shape and color, to dose the germ of future lilies with atmospheric and solar influence." [70]

Yet the observer must inevitably fail to understand the organization, the true beauty, of such an object as the lily, said Greenough, so long as he considers it literally. "The sublime," he argued, "is no quality in things, having a positive existence, but a *mental perception of relation*." [71] It is only, argued Greenough, through this mental perception of relation that the mind of man can read in nature those pronouncements of Deity of which organization is the utterance. Such pronouncements, he added, are not to be caught readily by the deaf ear of literal-minded inquiry. "Organization," he said, "has a language of its own," [72] encompassing "the entire gamut of visual qualities in objects." [73] It is a "language, a tongue," furthermore, "whose vocabulary must be learned, word by word." [74]

Unfortunately, he observed, the dicta of esthetical experts in regard to this language of natural forms represent, in the main, attempts to obstruct understanding, to confuse, rather than to clarify, the syntax of the language. "Finding in God's world a sensuous beauty not organically demonstrated to us," he said, "the hierarchies call on us to shut our eyes and kneel to an aesthetical utterance of the divinity." But, he added, "I refuse. Finding here an apparent embellishment, I consider the appearance of embellishment an accusation of ignorance and incompleteness in my science." [75]

Like Emerson, Greenough looked to science and to the improvement of his own "science," for aid in apprehending the structure of true unity, of true completeness, in nature as well as in art. "I call . . . upon science in all its branches," he said, "to arrest the tide of sensuous and arbitrary embellishment, so far as it can do it, not negatively by criticism thereof alone, but positively by making the instrument [that is, art] a many-sided response to the multiform demands of life. The craving for completeness will then obtain its normal food in results, not the opiate and the deadening stimulus of decoration." [76] And, like Emerson, Greenough called upon science for aid because he saw that

"God's law," being "as far away from our taste as his ways are beyond our ways," [77] requires all the aids to its interpretation which intellect, which science, can offer. Thus, in turning to nature Greenough sought, after the manner of the scientist, to "learn principles" rather than to "copy shapes." [78] "We shall seek in vain," he said, "to borrow shapes; we must *make* the shapes, and can only effect this by mastering the principles." [79]

As a result of this turning to nature in search of organization (of God's utterance) revealed in terms of principle, Greenough arrived eventually at appreciably the same awareness of the adaptation of structures to functions among organic forms as did Emerson. "If," he wrote, "as the first step in our search after the great principles of construction, we but observe the skeletons and skins of animals, through all the varieties of beast and bird, of fish and insect, are we not as forcibly struck by their variety as by their beauty? There is no arbitrary law of proportion, no unbending model of form. There is scarce a part of the animal organization which we do not find elongated or shortened, increased, diminished, or suppressed, as the wants of the genus or species dictate, as their exposure or their work may require." [80] And his conclusion was: "The law of adaptation is the fundamental law of nature in all structure." [81] Indeed, he said, "If there be any principle of structure more plainly inculcated in the works of the Creator than all others, it is the principle of unflinching adaptation of forms to functions." [82]

Accordingly, Greenough saw that the specific duties of the true artist were, first of all, to master this natural principle which governs the relationship between form and function; having mastered it, to learn the true function of each art object; and knowing that, to apply natural principle to the creation of the form or forms uniquely suited to that function. Subordinate forms were to be graded and organized in accordance with their relative significance in relation to the total function of the aggregate object. For "in art, as in nature," said Greenough, "the soul, the purpose of a work will never fail to be proclaimed in that work in proportion to the subordination of the parts to the whole, of the whole to the function." [83] Only thus, he argued, might the artist produce objects characterized by that true completeness, that true beauty, that cosmical relationship of unity, which transcends the bare object and connects with all things. Only then might the art of men achieve the beauty and majesty which characterize the eagle; for "it is the oneness of his function that gives him his grandeur, it is transcendental mechanism alone that begets his beauty." [84]

Thus it becomes apparent that to Greenough's mind the decisive element contributing to the achievement of a valid esthetic, and ultimately to the creation of true completeness and of true beauty in art, lay implicit in the artist's and in the critic's consideration of art forms in terms of function. It was this alone that might effect among art forms those aspects of organic and cosmic unity (or completeness) for which Green-

ough, as well as Emerson, yearned. Greenough even
went so far in this direction as to assert: "There is no
conceivable function which does not obey an absolute
law. The approximation to that law in material, in
parts, in their form, color, and relations, is the measure
of freedom or obedience to God, in life." [85] He went so
far, in short, as to conceive of the law of adaptation of
form to function as the supreme law, not only of biological forms in nature, but of God's universe as well.

From this position he went on to define beauty itself
in terms of function, rather than in terms of unity as
Emerson had done. "By beauty," said Greenough, "I
mean the promise of function." [86] Yet here again, the
differences between Greenough's conception of beauty
and Emerson's are more nearly differences of emphasis
than of essence; they result from the different manners
in which they are stated. Greenough and Emerson
were both, it will be remembered, concerned with
unity (or completeness) conceived cosmically, just as
they were both concerned with unity (or completeness) conceived organically, that is, in terms of adaptation. The difference between their two statements of
faith, as reflected specifically in their definitions of
beauty, lies in Emerson's subordination of the conception of adaptation to that of unity, in contrast with
Greenough's emphasis upon functional adaptation
somewhat to the neglect of his previously declared
goal of completeness.

Emerson's definition of beauty was more inclusive
than Greenough's, and Greenough seems to have been

aware of the inadequacy of his own definition. "To many minds," he conceded, "the definition of beauty as the promise of function must appear an excessive generalization. . . . Yet is this generalization but an effort to grasp a wider collection of phenomena, and, if developed, it is not certain that it will prove other than a step to a wider and a higher generalization." [87] However, in thus extending the emphasis he had placed upon the functional aspect of his esthetic conception, Greenough did not at the same time expand his statement to include his own key conception of completeness; and as a consequence he came to see not only beauty but even action and character in terms of function:

"Three things," he wrote, "I have seen in man worthy of . . . love and thought. Three proofs do I find in man that he was made only a little lower than the angels—Beauty—Action—Character.

"By Beauty I mean the promise of Function.

"By Action I mean the presence of Function.

"By Character I mean the record of Function." [88]

He came finally to see these three aspects of function as the principal agent-elements of normal development among all organized forms, and concluded, accordingly: "If the normal development of organized life be from beauty to action, from action to character, the progress is upward as well as forward; and action will be higher than beauty, . . . and character will be higher than action . . . If this be true, the attempt to prolong the phase of beauty into the epoch of action can only be made through nonperformance; and false beauty or embellishment must be the result. . . . The sensuous charm of promise is so great that the unripe reason seeks to make life a perennial promise; but promise, in the phase of action, receives a new name —that of nonperformance, and is visited with contempt." [89]

Life as well as art, then, conceived in terms progressively of promise of function, performance of function, and record of function, constituted, to Greenough's mind, the only true assurance of a mature esthetic and a mature art; and ignorance of such conceptions of function was to him equally the assurance of an incomplete esthetic and of an art characterized by false beauty—divorced from life and from the God-principle. For to one without these conceptions of function, said Greenough, "beauty may be present, yet not recognized as such. If we lack the sense of promise of function, beauty for us will not exist." [90] Yet none of these three major aspects of function stood completely alone in Greenough's mind. "When," he said, "I define beauty as the promise of function, . . . I arbitrarily divide that which is essentially one." [91] It was by means of this qualification, apparently, that Greenough sought to readmit the conception of unity into his definition of beauty.

It would probably be neither wise nor safe, in view of this last remark of Greenough's, to assert unqualifiedly that his pronouncement of that unitarian esthetic which he and Emerson held in common was more thoroughly thought out in all respects than Emerson's. Greenough was not the expansive type of thinker that Emerson was. He was not, for one thing, concerned so directly with those problems regarding the nature of thought, of language, and of the exact psychology of esthetic perception as was Emerson; and, being less concerned with such matters, he saw less clearly their bearing on his own particular problem. Hence, although Greenough was no mean esthetician by anybody's standard, it must be admitted that he was not so complete a philosopher as Emerson.

The question arises immediately upon this admission: Why, then, was Greenough more eloquent than Emerson? We shall find an answer as we examine Greenough's application of his unitarian esthetic theory to an assessment of the creative process.

5. THE ORGANIC PROCESS: A PRACTICAL METAPHYSICS OF ART

Greenough, being more a professional artist than a philosopher, came to deal more directly than Emerson did with the practical mechanics of the creative process —with the working metaphysics of art deriving from his organic esthetic. Emerson, more a philosopher than an artist, concerned himself principally with the theory of esthetic perception which lay half submerged beneath his primary concern with unity both in art and in the cosmos. Greenough, as Professor Matthiessen has suggested, arrived therefore at practical conclusions about creating unity in art which were beyond Emerson's scope. Greenough, accordingly, was more eloquent than Emerson because he offered to the aspiring young artist not vast speculations about the nature of the universe or of the human mind, but practical suggestions about what the artist should do.

To this effect, Greenough advised that art must be organized not only with esthetic intent but also with serious regard for the fact that always in the past "actual approximation to beauty has been effected, first, by strict adaptation of forms to functions, second, by the gradual elimination of all that is irrelevant and impertinent." [92] "The aim of the artist," he said, "should be first to seek the essential; when the essential hath been found, then, if ever, will be the time to commence embellishment." And he added: "I will venture to predict that the essential, when found, will be complete." [93]

It is worth noting that Greenough's statement includes not only a positive assertion but its contrapositive or negative statement as well. It not only implies, but says explicitly, that to agree to seek the essential is to agree equally to abandon the inessential. Greenough, of course, was not the first transcendental esthetician to match a positive statement of the organic principle with its negative assertion; Emerson had done so,[94] as also had Thoreau, who appears, in fact, to have made the negative statement the dominant one in his own conception. But Greenough was the first to apply both statements, with any real effect, to an assessment of the creative process as applied to his own or allied arts. Indeed, Greenough's further contribution to the organic esthetic, beyond his pronouncement of its principles in terms of specific actions to be undertaken by the artist, lay in his pointing up certain important areas of American culture in which these things which he advised the artist to do were actually being done. It lay in his showing, as he had hoped to show, that artistically Americans had done more "in the right direction" [95] than had been appreciated.

In Washington, Greenough found little confirmation of his esthetic theory—little evidence that the processes of seeking out the essential, or of eliminating the inessential, had been applied to the organization of forms. Such buildings as were elegant and satisfying were so, as often as not, because their forms and embellishments had been borrowed from the Greeks; whatever of elegance and satisfaction accrued to them was residual, carried over through the sheer genius of the original designers to impress the taste of the modern vulgarian. This second-hand art, it will be remembered, was precisely that which Greenough sought to replace. He saw, nevertheless, that it could teach a valuable lesson: "If . . . it shall have appeared that we regard the Greek masters as aught less than the true apostles of correct taste in building," he wrote, "we have been misunderstood. We believe firmly and fully that they can teach us; but let us learn principles, not copy shapes; let us imitate them like men, and not ape them like monkeys." [96] The Greeks, then, to Greenough's mind, were excellent architects—indeed, "the true apostles of correct taste in building"—not because they were ancient, nor because the forms of their art were beautiful *per se,* but because, being Greeks, they had developed the forms of their art in accordance with principle—that is, in accordance largely with natural principle. Hence he said, "I contend for Greek principles, not Greek things."

In this regard, however, Greenough was aware that whatever the Greeks might have taught the American artist had been so completely distorted by the literal-minded misinterpretations of neoclassic authority as to nullify its real value. Accordingly, in seeking illustration of their lesson he turned to other artisans, also guided by principle, who—living closer to nature even than the Greeks did, among even simpler circumstances, yet in modern times—could supply the inspiration necessary to the artist in search of true, dynamic, beauty in art. He turned to the primitive artisan, the noble savage, the natural man. "When," he observed, "the savage of the South Sea islands shapes his war club, his first thought is of its use. His first efforts pare the long shaft, and mold the convenient handle; then the heavier end takes gradually the edge that cuts, while it retains the weight that stuns. . . . We admire its effective shape, its Etruscan-like quaintness, its graceful form and subtle outline, yet *we neglect the lesson it might teach.*" [97]

It was in pondering the lesson demonstrated by the club, in reflecting upon its wisdom in terms of modern culture, that Greenough arrived at a conclusion of major significance in the development of his esthetic. For, he continued, "If we compare the form of a newly invented machine with the perfected type of the same instrument, we observe [also], as we trace it through the phases of improvement, how weight is shaken off where strength is less needed, how functions are made to approach without impeding each other, how straight becomes curved, and the curve is straightened, till the straggling and cumbersome machine becomes the compact, effective, and beautiful engine." [98] He saw, in effect, that the mechanic, operating almost undisturbed by the dictates of tradition, was approximating more closely the intuitive, organic wisdom of the savage artisan (the wisdom, indeed, of the Greeks) than was the professional artist of his time who merely copied shapes. And he remarked, accordingly, that the American artist might do well to look to his own technology for suggestions on how to reform art.

"Let us now turn," he said, "to a structure of our own, one which, from its nature and uses, commands us to reject authority, and we shall find the result of the manly use of plain good sense, so like that of taste, and genius too, as scarce to require a distinctive title. Observe a ship at sea! Mark the majestic form of her hull as she rushes through the water, observe the graceful bend of her body, the gentle transition from round to flat, the grasp of her keel, the leap of her bows, the symmetry and rich tracery of her spars and rigging, and those grand wind muscles, her sails. Behold an organization second only to that of an animal, obedient as the horse, swift as the stag, and bearing the burden of a thousand camels from pole to pole! What academy of design, what research of connoisseurship, what imitation of the Greeks produced this marvel of construction? Here is the result of the study of man upon the great deep, where Nature spake of the laws of building, not in the feather and in the flower, but in winds and waves." [99]

The source of this organic beauty characteristic of the sailing ship was response upon the part of the designers to disciplines, to responsibilities, imposed by the functions of the clipper ship and the frigate. "Could we carry," he concluded, "into our civil architecture the responsibilities that weigh upon our shipbuilding, we should ere long have edifices as superior to the Parthenon, for the purposes that we require, as the *Constitution* or the *Pennsylvania* is to the galley of the Argonauts." [100]

Hence, although Greenough, like Emerson, considered commerce and the mercantile society to be the enemies of true art, he did not view manufacture or the technological society entirely in that light. In fact, as we have seen, he saw in the operations of the mechanic, of the shipbuilder, a much closer adherence to natural principle—to scientific law—than in the productions of the neoclassic artist. He perceived, furthermore, that the emancipation of art from what amounted to a commerce-borne traditionalism was not only implicit in the processes of a developing American technology, but was actually being initiated by those processes as they operated among forms developing, paradoxically, in response to commercial opportunity.

Particularly, he remarked upon this revolutionary trend among such productions of technology as nowadays are entrusted to engineers. "In all structure that from its nature is purely scientific—in fortifications, in bridges, in shipbuilding—we have been emancipated from authority by the stern organic requirements of the works. The modern wants spurned the traditional formula in these structures, as the modern life outgrew the literary molds of Athens. In all these structures character has taken the place of dilettantism, and if we have yet to fight for sound doctrine in all structure, it is only because a doctrine which has possession must be expelled, inch by inch, however unsound its foundation." [101]

Since the mechanic, the engineer, the shipwright, had already indicated the direction which the artist should take in emancipating his art—since they had even advanced in that direction farther than the artist, —it was patently the responsibility of the artist, of the esthetician, as Greenough saw it, to apply the sound doctrine inherent in the mechanic's and in the shipbuilder's art to all other forms, including the architectural.

"What a field of study would be opened," he remarked, "by the adoption in civil architecture of those laws of apportionment, distribution, and connection which we have hinted at? No longer could the mere tyro huddle together a crowd of ill-arranged, ill-lighted, and stifled rooms and, masking the chaos with the sneaking copy of a Greek façade, usurp the name of architect. If this anatomic connection and proportion has been attained in ships, in machines, and, in spite of false principles, in such buildings as make a departure from it fatal, as in bridges and in scaffolding, why should we fear its immediate use in all construction? As its first result, the bank would have the physiognomy of a bank, the church would be recognized as such, nor would the billiard room and the chapel wear the same uniform of columns and pediment." [102]

"I would fain beg any architect who allows fashion to invade the domain of principles to compare the American vehicles and ships with those of England, and he will see that the mechanics of the United States have already outstripped the artists, and have, by the results of their bold and unflinching adaptation, entered the true track, and hold up the light for all who operate for American wants, be they what they will." [103]

"The men who have reduced locomotion to its simplest elements, in the trotting wagon and the yacht *America,* are nearer to Athens at this moment than they who would bend the Greek temple to every use. . . . If a flat sail goes nearest wind, a bellying sail, though picturesque, must be given up. The slender harness and tall gaunt wheels are not only effective, they are beautiful—for they respect the beauty of a horse, and do not uselessly task him. The English span is a good one, but they lug along more pretension than beauty . . . and

[are] therefore easily passed by those who care not to seem, but are." [104]

"Far be it from me," said Greenough, however, "to pretend that the style pointed out by our mechanics is what is sometimes miscalled an economical, a cheap style. No! it is the dearest of all styles! It costs the thought of men, much, very much thought, untiring investigation, ceaseless experiment. Its simplicity is not the simplicity of emptiness or of poverty; its simplicity is that of justness, I had almost said, of justice." [105] Its simplicity, Greenough might have added, is that of true completeness in both the organic and the cosmic sense. That completeness, as Greenough himself noted, does not just happen in art, but has to be thought out and built into each and every form. It is not a primitive completeness, however intuitively the savage ordnancer may apprehend it, but rather one which results, at the level of present culture, from highly ordered intellectual effort. It is, furthermore, not readily apparent to the literal-minded. And being far removed from the surface manifestations of things, it requires ample illustration, in art as well as in nature, if its significance is to be widely understood.

Adequate illustration, requiring as it does the invention of radically new art forms, is not easy. It was, in fact, beyond Greenough's powers of invention. He was forced, therefore, by his own inadequacy, to admit that "unfortunately for us the appreciation of an aesthetical theory without substantial art is as difficult as to follow a geometric demonstration without a diagram. It is sterile and impotent, as is all faith without work." [106]

Production of a substantial art necessary to the illustration of Greenough's theory was too large a job to be accomplished concurrently with the formulation of the theory itself. "The system of building we have hinted at," he said, "cannot be formed in a day. . . . Each of these requisites to a good building requires a special study and a lifetime. Whether we are destined soon to see so noble a fruit may be doubted; but we can, at least, break the ground and throw in the seed." [107] He would therefore "encourage experiment at the risk of license, rather than submit to an iron rule that begins by sacrificing reason, dignity, and comfort. Let us consult nature, and in the assurance that she will disclose a mine, richer than was ever dreamed of by the Greeks, in art as well as in philosophy." [108] For "the significance of yesterday, today, and tomorrow is this," he said, "that we are in a state of development." [109] It was the duty of the artist, of the esthetician, as Greenough saw it, to guarantee that forms should proceed always from a lower to a higher development.

Being aware, however, of his inability to secure this advancement through the production of significantly new forms, he found it necessary to discharge his duty as an artist by some other means—by those, namely, which were open to him as a seer and as a prophet of the transcendental organic esthetic. His assumption of this role was entirely consistent with the general protestant religious tenor of his esthetic faith; for the protestant believer is more often a seer, or visionary, than not—and quite often he becomes a prophet. Greenough's role was a novel one since his vision and prophecy were applied to esthetic rather than to religious protest. Yet it was not unique, for it was a role which he shared, as he shared his esthetic faith, in company with Emerson.

CONCLUSION

Superior vision often functions negatively as a source of protest and a guide to criticism. But vision has its positive as well as its negative manifestations. And if the negative manifestations of insight give utterance in the forms of protest and of criticism, the positive manifestations also announce themselves, if not in action, at least in prophecy. Prophecy is generally conducted in one of three major ways: by announcement, by prediction, and sometimes by sponsorship. Both Emerson and Greenough were in some degree prophets: each announced the results of his superior insight at some length both in writings and in lectures. In prediction Greenough was more active than Emerson, foreseeing in the application of the organic esthetic to architecture the achievement finally of such true completeness in man's art as is characteristic of nature's forms, and as is demonstrated today in our better modern architecture.

Greenough, unfortunately, saw no champion capable of fulfilling his prophecy, found in his lifetime no disciple to give substance to his prediction. Emerson, on the other hand, found several champions to supply some evidence in confirmation of his esthetic faith—in confirmation of his hope for the development of art toward the attainment of true beauty. Greenough, ironically, was one of these champions; Whitman was another. That Whitman was for a time at least Emerson's disciple—that Emerson was, in effect, his sponsor —is common enough knowledge. Even if Whitman had arrived at the point of simmering without Emerson's help, it was the older poet, after all, who brought the younger one to a boil. And Whitman's admission of this connection establishes measurably his status as Emerson's heir.

Greenough's heirs, however, apparently never heard of him. They did not arrive upon the scene until some fifty years after his death and the publication of his collected writings. Both the man and his work seem soon to have been forgotten, and long remained so; his essays were not reprinted until 1947. Yet when, in the eighteen eighties, the "Chicago school" of architects (specifically Adler, Sullivan, and Wright) did apply to their art what amounted in essence to Greenough's esthetic, the results were quite as revolutionary in kind as those of Whitman in his earlier application of a similar esthetic to poetry.

Emerson and Greenough, then, mark each in his own way the beginnings of parallel traditions in literature and architecture—traditions which may be traced, with occasional breaks in sequence, right up to the present. Emerson by way of his general philosophical theories of nature, and Greenough by way of his more specific studies of form in relation to natural function, both arrived at essentially the same advanced conclusions—which, incidentally, are considered "modern" today.

Honor, accordingly, is due both Emerson and Greenough, who, fifty years in advance of the present enthusiasm for the organic esthetic, inaugurated with their pronouncements what has since become one of the more important trends in the history of American art.

NOTES

Notes to Chapter One (pp. 5–23)

[1] *Writings,* Vol. V, p. 54. My italics.

[2] The term *philosophy* is used here to connote the process of free inquiry, rather than the process of rigid indoctrination which so often characterizes the action of institutions newly come or coming to relatively complete control over society.

[3] *Main Currents in American Thought,* Vol. II, p. 381.

[4] "Art," *Works,* Vol. I, p. 354.

[5] In the same essay Emerson says (p. 355), "We call the Beautiful the highest, because it appears to us the golden mean, escaping the dowdiness of the good and the heartlessness of the true."

[6] *Journals,* Vol. IV, p. 76.

[7] *Ibid.,* Vol. VI, p. 25.

[8] *Works,* p. 4.

[9] *Journals,* Vol. II, p. 178.

[10] I define the term *institution* here in its broadest sense, as an agreement among men to do or to refrain from doing more or less consistently a certain thing or things over any considerable period of time.

[11] See William Warren Sweet's chapter entitled "Religion Reaches the Masses: The Great Awakening," in *Religion in Colonial America.*

[12] *Works,* Vol. I, p. 335.

[13] Having gone to nature to commune with Deity, the transcendentalist appears to have remained there to observe God's handiwork, and to have emerged as something of a natural scientist. By this analogy we see Emerson the communicant as having entered the woods behind Concord and as having remained there, half communicant, half observer. And by the same analogy we recognize Thoreau emerging more the observer, more the skeptic, more the naturalist, than the communicant who went in.

Notes to Chapter Two (pp. 24–66)

[1] *Main Currents in American Thought,* Vol. II, p. 384.

[2] *Works,* Vol. 1, p. 339.

[3] *American Renaissance,* p. xv.

[4] "Art," *Works,* Vol. II, p. 368.

[5] "Beauty," *ibid.,* Vol. VI, p. 292.

[6] "Art," *ibid.,* Vol. II, p. 368.

[7] "Beauty," *ibid.,* Vol. VI, p. 294. It is fitting to mention at this point an article by Robert B. Shaffer, "Emerson and His Circle: Advocates of Functionalism," in the *Journal of the Society of Architectural Historians.* Mr. Shaffer takes note of Emerson's saying, in his *Dial* article "Thoughts on Art," which was reprinted in *Society and Solitude* (*Works,* Vol. VI, pp. 37–57): "Arising out of eternal reason, one and perfect, whatever is beautiful rests on the foundation of the necessary. . . . Fitness is so inseparable an accompaniment of beauty, that it has been taken for it. The most perfect form to answer an end, is so far beautiful." Mr. Shaffer also directs attention to an article, "Notes on Art and Architecture," by Samuel Gray Ward, an amateur draftsman and art connoisseur, which was published in the *Dial,* Vol. IV (1843), pp. 105–115, when Emerson had become the editor of that magazine; and an article, "Notes on Domestic Architecture," by James Elliot Cabot, who was for a time an architect, which appeared in the *Atlantic Monthly,* Vol. I (1858), pp. 257–263. Cabot's article included the sentence: ". . . a house is not a monument, that it should draw attention to itself,—but the dwelling-place of men upon the earth; and it must show itself to be wholly secondary to its purpose."

[8] "Beauty," *Works,* Vol. VI, p. 294. The phrase "line of beauty" is Hogarth's, and was once widely known and discussed. Hogarth meant by it a waving line, which he declared was "more productive of beauty" than straight, circular, or other regularly drawn lines or combinations of them. He praised it as ornamental, but did not argue for it as "economical"; in the opening chapter of his *Analysis of Beauty* (1753) he discussed fitness as an element of beauty, though not specifying it as functional (as Greenough was to do) and not founding upon fitness a definite esthetic (as Greenough was to found one upon function, which *is* economical).

[9] "Beauty," *Works,* Vol. VI, p. 291.

[10] *Journals,* Vol. IV, pp. 115–116.

[11] *Ibid.,* Vol. X, p. 236.

[12] *Ibid.*, Vol. IV, p. 436. Emerson's italics.

[13] *Ibid.*, Vol. X, p. 236.

[14] *Works,* Vol. VI, p. 304.

[15] *Ibid.*, p. 289.

[16] *Ibid.*

[17] Thomas Aquinas has a version of the same thing in his *Summa contra Gentiles,* Bk. III, Pt. I, chap. xxv: "The operation proper to a thing is the end thereof: for it is its second perfection; so that when a thing is well conditioned for its proper operation it is said to be efficient and good." In chap. xxvi he adds: "The right order of things agrees with the order of nature: for in the natural order things are directed to their end without any error. . . . In the natural order delight is on account of operation and not conversely." These quotations are from *The Summa contra Gentiles* literally translated by the English Dominican Fathers, Bk. III, Pt. I, pp. 56, 64.

[18] "Art," *Works,* Vol. II, p. 355.

[19] "Beauty," *ibid.*, Vol. VI, p. 303.

[20] *Journals,* Vol. V, p. 537.

[21] *Ibid.*, Vol. IV, pp. 270–271.

[22] "Art," *Works,* Vol. II, p. 367.

[23] "The Poet," *Works,* Vol. III, p. 3.

[24] *Journals,* Vol. V, p. 488.

[25] *Ibid.*, Vol. VII, p. 33.

[26] *Works,* Vol. II, p. 353. Emerson's italics.

[27] *Ibid.*, p. 354.

[28] *Ibid.*, p. 366.

[29] *Ibid.*, p. 367.

[30] *Ibid.*, p. 365.

[31] *Ibid.*, p. 363.

[32] *Journals,* Vol. IV, p. 102.

[33] "Art," *Works,* Vol. II, p. 363.

[34] *Ibid.*, p. 351.

[35] *Ibid.*, pp. 362–363.

[36] *Ibid.*, p. 365.

[37] *Journals,* Vol. VIII, p. 125. My italics.

[38] *Works,* Vol. II, p. 19.

[39] *Ibid.*

[40] *Ibid.*

[41] *Ibid.* Compare the foregoing statement with the following from Milizia's *Lives of Celebrated Architects* (pp. xv–xvi), which Emerson is quite likely to have read: "If the Greeks were the first imitators of architecture, that is, of the art and science of building, what path did

they pursue to arrive at so noble a termination? Cottages could have been the only model. It is therefore apparent, that they must have imitated these in stone. . . . Trunks of trees vertically placed to support the roofs of the first habitations, were easily converted to stone columns. . . . From the covering or roof of the hut overhanging, arise the fastigi, called pediments, which were made more or less acute, according to the nature of the climate." Georg Moller, whom Emerson cites (see p. 78 *supra*), also made an assertion similar to this last one of Milizia's (in his *Denkmäler der deutschen Baukunst,* 1815) regarding the influence of climate on the pitch of the Gothic roof and hence of the Gothic arch. The present and all subsequent quotations from Milizia are from Mrs. Edward Cresy's translation (1826) of his *Memorie degli architetti antichi e moderni.*

[42] *Works,* Vol. I, pp. 85–86.

[43] "History," *ibid.,* Vol. II, p. 15.

[44] *Journals,* Vol. III, p. 517.

[45] *Ibid.,* Vol. IX, pp. 424–425.

[46] *Ibid.,* p. 528.

[47] "Beauty," *Works,* Vol. VI, p. 290.

[48] That Emerson was influenced early, particularly by the emergent biological sciences of his day, shows in his *Journal* entry of 1833 (at age 30) occasioned by his visit to the Jardin des Plantes in Paris. "Not a form so grotesque, so savage, nor so beautiful," he said, "but is an expression of some property inherent in man the observer,—an occult relation between the very scorpions and man. I feel the centipede in me,—cayman, carp, eagle, and fox. I am moved by strange sympathies; I say continually, 'I will be a naturalist.'" *Journals,* Vol. III, p. 163.

[49] "Biographical Sketch" (by Edward Waldo Emerson), *Works,* Vol. I, p. xviii. Lamarck's four basic laws are: "1. Life, by its own forces, tends continually to increase the volume of every body that possesses life, and to enlarge the dimensions of that body's parts, up to a limit which life itself brings about. 2. The production of a new organ in an animal body results from the supervention of a new want that continues to make itself felt, and of a new movement to which this want gives birth and which it encourages. 3. The development of organs and their force of action are constantly in proportion to the employment of those organs. 4. All that has been acquired, laid down, or changed in the organization of individuals, in the course of their life, is conserved by generation and transmitted to the new individuals which proceed from those which have undergone these

changes." (Introduction to Lamarck's *Histoire naturelle des animaux sans vertèbres*, 1815; 2d ed., 1835, Vol. I, pp. 151–152.)

[50] See p. 53 *supra*.

[51] "In happy hours, nature appears to us one with art; art perfected, —the work of genius," said Emerson in his essay on "Art," *Works*, Vol. II, p. 358.

[52] Of genius, Emerson wrote in his *Journals*, Vol. IV, p. 253: "Creation is always the style and act of these minds."

[53] *Journals*, Vol. X, p. 467.

[54] *Ibid.*, Vol. III, p. 474.

[55] "Poetry and Imagination," *Works*, Vol. VIII, pp. 17–18.

[56] *Journals*, Vol. I, p. 313.

[57] *Ibid.*, Vol. VI, pp. 370–371.

[58] *Ibid.*, Vol. IV, pp. 252–253. My italics.

[59] See p. 61 and note 51, *supra*.

[60] "Art," *Works*, Vol. II, p. 368.

[61] *Ibid.*, p. 364.

[62] *Ibid.*, p. 356.

Notes to Chapter Three (pp. 67–79)

[1] Lorado Taft, *The History of American Sculpture*, p. 51.

[2] *American Renaissance*, p. 144.

[3] Taft, *op. cit.*, p. 53.

[4] The relationship between Cooper's thought and Greenough's is at times surprisingly close. Thus in Cooper's American *roman de société*, *Home as Found* (1838), one of the characters remarks in the very first chapter that "public sentiment just now runs almost exclusively and popularly to the Grecian school"; adding wryly, "We build little besides temples for our churches, our banks, our taverns, our court-houses, and our dwellings. A friend of mine has just built a brewery on the model of the Temple of the Winds." In chapter viii the subject is taken up again: "The fault just now is perhaps to consult the books too rigidly, and to trust too little to invention; for no architecture, and especially no domestic architecture, can ever be above serious reproach, until climate, the uses of the edifice, and the situation, are respected as leading considerations. Nothing can be uglier, *per se*, than a Swiss cottage, or anything more beautiful under its precise circumstances. As regards these mushroom temples which are the offspring of Mammon, let them be dedicated to whom they may,

I should exactly reverse the opinion and say, that while nothing can be much more beautiful *per se,* nothing can be in worse taste than to put them where they are." And in Cooper's last novel, *The Ways of the Hour* (1850), chap. xxi, one of his characters complains: "Every town is getting its Broadway, thus defeating the very object of names; to-day the country is dotted with Grecian temples, to-morrow with Gothic villages, all the purposes of domestic architecture being sadly forgotten in each . . ." Compare these remarks with Greenough's on the same subject, this volume, pp. 101 and 129 f.

[5] Henry T. Tuckerman, *Book of the Artists: American Artist Life . . .* (1867).

[6] Taft, *op. cit.,* p. 38.

[7] *Ibid.,* p. 54.

[8] *Ibid.,* p. 55. Greenough did most of his work in Florence.

[9] *Journals,* Vol. VIII, p. 390, quoted from *The Correspondence of . . . Carlyle and . . . Emerson,* Vol. II, p. 219.

[10] *Works,* Vol. XII, p. 223.

[11] *The Travels, Observations, and Experience of a Yankee Stone-cutter,* pp. 63–64.

[12] *Journals,* Vol. III, p. 146.

[13] *Ibid.,* p. 147.

[14] *Works,* Vol. II, p. 359.

[15] *Ibid.,* Vol. V, pp. 5–6. Emerson's italics. There is no record of Greenough's actually having read Lamarck; yet certainly, as the passage above suggests, Greenough was exposed to his or to similar ideas.

[16] "Fate," Works, Vol. VI, p. 45: "Möller [*sic*], in his Essay on Architecture, taught that the building which was fitted accurately to answer its end would turn out to be beautiful though beauty had not been intended." I have been unable to locate this essay, unless it is *An Essay on the Origin and Progress of Gothic Architecture . . . ,* translated from the German (London, 1824), which is taken from Moller's *Denkmäler der deutschen Baukunst* (1815). The teaching mentioned by Emerson is not specifically so stated in this English book, but may have been "read into it" by Emerson.

[17] *American Renaissance,* p. 136.

[18] "It was too bad," says Matthiessen (*op. cit.,* pp. 153–154), "that Thoreau's prickly reaction against anything proposed by Emerson . . . should have kept him from appreciating that in Greenough he had a natural ally whose maturer thought could have guided his own."

NOTES TO CHAPTER FOUR (pp. 80–133)

[1] This book (published by G. P. Putnam, New York) was offered by its author pseudonymously, as "by Horace Bender." Its first chapter, "Aesthetics at Washington," had been published separately (printed by Jno. T. Towers, Washington, D.C., 1851), and others of its parts had appeared in magazines and newspapers. Some of its chapters had first been presented as public lectures by the author.

[2] *Travels*, p. vii. "Your thought-bred gentleman and scholar," said Greenough, "utters his compliment or his opinion with abandon, yet well and gracefully. I can't do this in my book, and shall not try to seem like those who can. I shall endeavor to be clear, clean and civil, which is all I can promise."

[3] *A Memorial of Horatio Greenough, Consisting of a Memoir, Selections from His Writings, and Tributes to His Genius* (New York, G. P. Putnam, 1853).

[4] *Form and Function: Remarks on Art by Horatio Greenough*, edited by Harold A. Small, with an Introduction by Erle Loran (Berkeley and Los Angeles, University of California Press, 1947).

[5] The phrase quoted is from Professor Loran's Introduction, *Form and Function*, p. xiii.

[6] See especially his essay on "Relative and Independent Beauty."

[7] As suggested briefly on pages 1 f. *supra*, there appears to have been developing in Europe a parallel esthetic tradition, the champions of which, Georg Moller (1784–1852) in Germany, Eugène-Emmanuel Viollet-le-Duc (1814–1879) in France, and Francesco Milizia (1725–1798) in Italy, may have provided Greenough as well as Emerson with some of the materials of their argument by way of contacts at present unknown. The earliest of these three, Milizia, of whom Mrs. Cresy (*op. cit.*) has observed "that his opinions have been more generally adopted than acknowledged" (p. viii), summarized these opinions as follows (pp. xviii–xx): "Architecture, like every other fine art, is subject to the following general rules: 1st, In all its productions there should be an agreeable relation between the parts and the whole; which is comprehended under the name of symmetry. 2nd, Variety, which prevents the object from becoming tiresome to the spectator; and unity, which prevents disorder and confusion, and is called eurythmy. 3rd, Convenience is necessary, then ornament, which makes a just use of symmetry and eurythmy, and of the relation

which there should be between an edifice and its destiny, and between the ornaments and quality of the building, adopting those most conformable to its magnificence, elegance, or simplicity. 4th, If architecture be the daughter of necessity, even its beauties should appear to result from such. In no part of the decoration should there be any artifice discoverable; hence, everything extraneous is a proof of bad taste. 5th, The principal features of architecture are its orders, or, more properly, they are the essentials of building; and are therefore considered as ornaments only when usefully placed: and all other architectural ornaments are subject to the same laws. 6th, Nothing must be introduced which has not its proper office, and is not an integral part of the fabric itself; so that whatever is represented must appear of service. 7th, No arrangement must be made for which a good reason cannot be assigned. 8th, These reasons must be deduced from the origin and analysis of that primitive architecture, of the cottage, which, as we before observed, was the origin of civil architecture. This is the directing rule of artists in their work, and of the learned in the examining of them. Everything must be founded upon truth or its similitude. Whatever cannot really and truly exist, cannot be approved of in representation. 9th, Examples and authority, however great they may be, should have no effect on the reason."

[8] *Letters of Horatio Greenough to His Brother . . . ,* p. 142.

[9] This is presumably the paper to which Emerson referred—the paper entitled "American Architecture," which had made its first appearance in the *United States Magazine and Democratic Review,* Vol. XIII (1843), pp. 206–210, and which became chapter ix in Greenough's *Travels.*

[10] *Form and Function,* pp. 5–6.

[11] Greenough had lived almost continually in Italy from 1825 to 1851, returning betweentimes only in 1826 and 1842–1843.

[12] American literary art, furthermore, was not in such a bad way as the other arts.

[13] Greenough's "Rescue" was designed as its companion piece.

[14] *Form and Function,* p. 14.

[15] *Ibid.,* pp. 14–15.

[16] *Ibid.,* p. 15. A Baltimorean traveling in Spain in 1847 viewed regretfully the mutilated busts that ornamented the Alameda in Malaga, and when he wrote about his journey he was moved to remark upon vandalism as "one of our [American] weaknesses," incidentally suggesting an explanation for some of it. "The last time that I saw Greenough's colossal Washington, in the garden of the Capitol,"

he recalled, "some irreverent heathen had taken the pains to climb up and insert a large 'plantation' cigar between the lips of the *pater patriae,* while another had amused himself with writing some stanzas of poetry, in a style rather popular than elegant, upon a prominent part of the body of the infant Hercules, who is strangling serpents, in relief, upon the lower part of the work. I could not help thinking, at the time, that if Washington had looked less like the Olympic Jove, and more like himself, not even the vagabond who perpetrated the trick of the cigar would have dared or dreamed of such a desecration." S. T. Wallis, *Glimpses of Spain; or, Notes of an Unfinished Tour in 1847* (New York, 1849), pp. 81–82.

[17] *Form and Function,* pp. 15–16.

[18] *Ibid.,* p. 16.

[19] *Ibid.,* pp. 23–24.

[20] *Ibid.,* p. 26.

[21] *Ibid.,* pp. 27–28.

[22] *Ibid.,* p. 27. Greenough's italics.

[23] *Ibid.,* p. 30.

[24] *Ibid.,* p. 11.

[25] *Ibid.,* p. 12.

[26] *Ibid.,* p. 22.

[27] *Ibid.,* pp. 53–54.

[28] *Ibid.,* p. 54.

[29] *Ibid.,* p. 115.

[30] *Ibid.,* p. 17.

[31] *Ibid.,* p. 2.

[32] *Ibid.,* p. 64.

[33] *Ibid.,* p. 6.

[34] *Ibid.,* p. 3.

[35] *Ibid.*

[36] *Ibid.* With similar caution Milizia announced of his own country: "Italy may justly be said to possess not only the most sumptuous, but the most perfect buildings in Europe, or the world, and her architecture is superior to that of any other nation; but her superiority is more relative than positive. It is the superiority of those who have one eye over the totally blind. With regret it must be acknowledged, she has not, in latter days, made use of all the advantages she possesses." *The Lives of Celebrated Architects,* Vol. II, p. 399.

[37] *Form and Function,* pp. 56–57.

[38] *Ibid.,* pp. 115–116.

[39] *Ibid.,* p. 54.

[40] *Ibid.,* pp. 20–21.

[41] *Ibid.,* p. 116.

[42] *Ibid.,* pp. 20–21.

[43] *Ibid.,* p. 21.

[44] *Ibid.* Cf. Milizia's sixth rule (see note 7, above).

[45] *Form and Function,* p. 21.

[46] *Ibid.,* p. 43.

[47] *Ibid.,* p. 45.

[48] *Ibid.,* pp. 45–46.

[49] *Ibid.,* p. 48.

[50] *Ibid.,* p. 46.

[51] *Travels,* p. 94.

[52] *Form and Function,* pp. 35–36.

[53] *Ibid.,* p. 37.

[54] *Ibid.,* p. 26.

[55] *Ibid.,* p. 9.

[56] *Ibid.,* p. 50. (Possibly a reference to the National Academy of Design, founded in 1825.)

[57] *Ibid.,* p. 85.

[58] *Ibid.,* pp. 94–95.

[59] *Ibid.,* p. 77.

[60] *Ibid.,* pp. 73–74.

[61] *Ibid.,* p. 85.

[62] *Ibid.,* p. 99. Greenough's italics.

[63] *Ibid.,* p. 92.

[64] *Ibid.,* p. 82.

[65] *Ibid.,* p. 81. Cf. the following from Thomas Aquinas: "Thus the perfection of a house considered as already having its species, is that to which the species 'house' is directed, namely to be a dwelling: for one would not build a house but for that: . . . On the other hand the perfection that conduces to the species of a house, is both that which is directed to the *completion* of the species, for instance its essential principles; and that which conduces to the preservation of the species, for instance the buttresses which are made to support the building; and those things which make the house more fit for use, for instance the symmetry of the building." *Summa contra Gentiles,* Bk. III, Pt. I, chap. xxvi (p. 65 of the Dominican Fathers' translation). My italics.

[66] *Form and Function,* p. 81.

[67] *Ibid.,* p. 79.

[68] *Ibid.,* p. 74. My italics.

[69] *Ibid.,* p. 118.

[70] *Ibid.,* p. 76.

[71] *Ibid.,* p. 88. Greenough's italics.

[72] *Ibid.,* p. 122.

[73] *Ibid.,* p. 95.

[74] *Ibid.*

[75] *Ibid.,* p. 76.

[76] *Ibid.,* p. 86. In this passage, and elsewhere, Greenough's use of the term *science* suggests the older meaning, of science as organized knowledge, a meaning which includes, however, the present, more specific meaning. Milizia also, using *science* in this older sense, had announced: "The science of architecture we certainly owe to the Greeks; and it is theory and practice which constitute the principal difference between science and art. The latter is a system of knowledge, reduced to positive rule, invariable, and independent of caprice or opinion. Science is the knowledge of the relation which a certain number of facts have to each other, and necessarily supposes the previous existence and discovery of these facts." *The Lives of Celebrated Architects,* p. xiv.

[77] *Form and Function,* p. 71.

[78] *Ibid.,* p. 65.

[79] *Ibid.,* p. 123. My italics.

[80] *Ibid.,* pp. 57–58.

[81] *Ibid.,* p. 58.

[82] *Ibid.,* p. 118.

[83] *Ibid.,* p. 121.

[84] *Ibid.,* p. 119.

[85] *Ibid.,* p. 85.

[86] *Travels,* p. 187.

[87] *Form and Function,* p. 97.

[88] *Travels,* p. 187; cf. *Form and Function,* p. 71.

[89] *Form and Function,* p. 72.

[90] *Ibid.,* p. 80.

[91] *Ibid.,* p. 71.

[92] *Ibid.,* p. 122.

[93] *Ibid.,* pp. 80–81.

[94] Cf. Emerson's definition of beauty, pp. 57 f. *supra.*

[95] Cf. p. 99 *supra.*

[96] *Form and Function,* p. 65. Similarly Milizia: "When Greek architecture is thoroughly understood, our edifices will not only be less expensive in their construction but more beautiful, and more creditable to the artists themselves, as well as the whole nation"; but he complained that even in Italy Greek architecture was not thoroughly understood. *The Lives of Celebrated Architects,* Vol. II, p. 399.

[97] *Form and Function*, p. 59. My italics. Had the lesson been entirely neglected? Greenough might have recalled that Cooper had twice noted the beauty and efficiency of the American ax: in *Notions of the Americans* (1828), where he remarked that it was "admirable for form, for neatness, and precision of weight, and . . . wielded with a skill that is next to incredible"; and in chapter vi of *The Chainbearer* (1845), where he apostrophized at some length "this beautiful, well-prized, ready, and efficient implement."

[98] *Form and Function*, p. 59.

[99] *Ibid.*, pp. 60–61. It is interesting to note that Thomas Aquinas also considered the functional character of marine architecture: "Now in all sciences and arts," he said, "that are mutually subordinate, the last end apparently belongs to the one from which others take their rules and principles: thus the art of sailing, to which belongs the ship's end, namely its use, provides rules and principles to the art of ship-building." *Summa contra Gentiles*, Bk. III, Pt. I, chap. xxv (p. 59 of the Dominican Fathers' translation). And Hogarth, in his *Analysis of Beauty*, wrote: ". . . in ship-building the dimensions of every part are confined and regulated by fitness for sailing. When a vessel sails well, the sailors always call her *a beauty;* the two ideas have such a connection!"

[100] *Form and Function*, p. 61.
[101] *Ibid.*, pp. 116–117.
[102] *Ibid.*, pp. 62–63.
[103] *Ibid.*, p. 127.
[104] *Ibid.*, p. 22.
[105] *Ibid.*, p. 128.
[106] *Ibid.*, p. 2.
[107] *Ibid.*, p. 67.
[108] *Ibid.*, p. 57.
[109] *Ibid.*, p. 83.

BIBLIOGRAPHY

Channing, William Ellery. *The Works of William E. Channing, D.D.* (Boston, American Unitarian Association, 1875).

Cooper, James Fenimore. *The Chainbearer* (1845).

——. *Home As Found* (1838).

——. *The Travelling Bachelor; or, Notions of the Americans* (1828).

——. *The Ways of the Hour* (1850).

Emerson, Ralph Waldo. *The Complete Works . . .* , ed. Edward Waldo Emerson (Concord Edition, 12 vols.; Boston, Houghton Mifflin, 1903–1921).

——. *The Journals of Ralph Waldo Emerson,* ed. Edward Waldo Emerson and Waldo Emerson Forbes (10 vols.; Boston, Houghton Mifflin, 1909–1914).

Greenough, Horatio. *Letters of Horatio Greenough to His Brother, Henry Greenough,* ed. Frances Boott Greenough (Boston, Ticknor, 1887).

——. [Selections from his writings, in] *Form and Function: Remarks on Art by Horatio Greenough,* ed. Harold A. Small (Berkeley and Los Angeles, University of California Press, 1947).

——. [Selections from his writings, in] *A Memorial of Horatio Greenough, Consisting of a Memoir, Selections from His Writings, and Tributes to His Genius,* ed. Henry T. Tuckerman (New York, Putnam, 1853).

——. *The Travels, Observations, and Experience of a Yankee Stonecutter,* by Horace Bender [pseud.] (New York, Putnam, 1852).

Hogarth, William. *The Analysis of Beauty* (1753).

Matthiessen, F. O. *American Renaissance: Art and Experience in the Age of Emerson and Whitman* (New York, Oxford University Press, 1941).

Milizia, Francesco. *Le vite de' più celebri architetti* (Rome, 1768), reprinted under the title *Memorie degli architetti antichi e moderni* (Parma, 1781); English translation, *The Lives of Celebrated Architects,* by Mr. Edward Cresy (2 vols.; London, 1826).

Parrington, Vernon Louis. *Main Currents in American Thought* (3 vols.; New York, Harcourt, Brace, 1927–1930).

Shaffer, Robert B. "Emerson and His Circle: Advocates of Functionalism," *Journal of the Society of Architectural Historians,* Vol. VII, Nos. 3–4 (July–December, 1948), pp. 17–20.

Sweet, William Warren. *Religion in Colonial America* (New York, Scribner, 1942).

Taft, Lorado. *The History of American Sculpture* (New York, Macmillan, 1903; latest edition, 1930).

Thomas Aquinas. *The Summa contra Gentiles of Saint Thomas Aquinas,* literally translated by the English Dominican Fathers (4 vols. in 5; London, Burns, Oates & Washbourne, 1923–1929).

Tuckerman, Henry T. *Book of the Artists: American Artist Life . . .* (New York, Putnam, 1867).

INDEX

Action, 121
Adaptation, 33, 118
Antiquarian, 31, 32, 44, 46, 47, 49, 50–51, 102, 104
Architecture, 54, 59, 71–78, 80, 84, 85, 91–97 *passim*, 101–103, 129–130, 134, 135, 136, 143–144 n. 7
Ax, 148 n. 97

Banks, 49, 130, 141 n. 4
Beauty, 7, 13, 14–15, 23, 26–45 *passim*, 50, 52, 60, 61, 77, 80, 94, 96, 110–114 *passim*, 119, 120, 121, 126

Calvinism, 8, 19
Carlyle, Thomas, 70
Catholic, Catholicism, 6–7, 106–107
Channing, William Ellery, 6, 10, 16–17, 83
Character, 121
"Chicago school" of architects, 135
Commerce, commercial, 25, 46, 48, 96, 97, 128–129
Completeness, 111–121, 134–135
Conception, the expanded, 27–29, 34–36, 39
Cooper, James Fenimore, 68, 141–142 n. 4, 148 n. 97
Creation, 46, 52, 56, 57, 59, 62, 63–65, 81, 86, 141 n. 52
Critic, critical, 24–26, 42, 43, 82; criticism, 45–52, 94

Darwin, Charles, 34, 58
Decorums, 47

Deism, deists, 19–20, 21
Deity, 14–22 *passim*, 27–31, 34, 43, 44, 45, 50, 64. *See also* God
Dilettantism, 99–100, 129

Economy, 33, 77, 78
Egypt, Egyptian, 89–90, 97
Embellishment, 50, 74, 83, 102, 111, 112, 114, 116, 117, 122, 124. *See also* Ornament
Episcopalians, 19
Essential, the, 124

Fitness, 138 n. 7
Form, 22, 23, 33, 46, 51, 53, 54, 69, 74, 100, 118–119, 124, 136; forms of art, 32, 42, 46–49, 51, 53, 54, 64, 69, 113, 118, 119, 124, 125; forms of nature, 32, 36, 42, 52, 54, 113, 117
Function, 42, 44, 48, 49, 50, 74, 78, 92, 93, 100, 102–103, 111, 118–128 *passim*, 136

Genius, 60–66, 69, 85, 105, 106, 125, 141 n. 52
God, 10, 13, 16, 17–22 *passim*, 27–31 *passim*, 34–38 *passim*, 43–45 *passim*, 106, 109, 112, 115, 120, 122. *See also* Deity
Gothic, 54, 94, 99, 112, 140 n. 41, 142 n. 4
"Great Awakening," the, 19
Grecian, Greek, 49, 69, 89–90, 94, 100, 112, 126, 130, 141–142 n. 4; Greece, 50, 69, 93, 95, 97; Greeks, 73, 125–126, 127, 139–140 n. 41, 147 nn. 76 and 96